PALIMPSEST

PALIMPSEST

A History of the Written Word

MATTHEW BATTLES

W. W. NORTON & COMPANY

NEW YORK LONDON

For information about permission to reproduce selections from this book,
write to Permissions, W. W. Norton & Company, Inc.,
500 Fifth Avenue, New York, NY 10110

For information about special discounts for bulk purchases, please contact
W. W. Norton Special Sales at specialsales@wwnorton.com or 800-233-4830

Manufacturing by Courier Westford
Book design by Love Dog Studio
Production manager: Louise Mattarelliano

ISBN: 978-0-393-05885-7

W. W. Norton & Company, Inc., 500 Fifth Avenue, New York, NY 10110
www.wwnorton.com

W. W. Norton & Company Ltd., Castle House, 75/76 Wells Street, London W1T 3QT

1 2 3 4 5 6 7 8 9 0

Contents

PALIMPSEST

MIND AS PAGE

I am left-handed, and my first-grade teacher didn't know what to do with me. The Palmer Method handwriting books, which many will recall in a haze of nostalgia and revulsion, were authored in a right-handed world, where paper was always tilted counterclockwise and pencils were never pushed, but only pulled. We should understand these methods as the introduction of ethics into the body, a set of orthodoxies to be performed, ablution-like, over the production of sacred text. Only my body, however subtly, was arranged according to a different order and would not respond to Miss W's ethical demands: Keep your back straight, adjust the paper to the proper angle, hold the pencil with gentle pressure—normative injunctions with the force of the Decalogue or the Golden Rule. Despite the admonishments—and despite the multicolored variety of rubber appliances and prostheses affixed to my pencils—I persisted in hooking my wrist, turning the paper the wrong way, and giving my apprentice characters a reprobate slouch and a blurry smudge. Where it had slid across the paper, the meat of my left hand glowed with the dull shine of graphite.

I soldiered on, however—for even before I could read or write, the letters of the alphabet had achieved fixed and peculiar characters known only to me: the letter *M*, for instance, was clearly brown—a low-nosed, snuffling, square-bodied beast. *H* was a house, alliteratively enough, black and strong, with room enough for all the other letters if it rained. As for *A*, which was white as distance itself, it was clearly a pair of railroad tracks receding—or sometimes, the house of *H* seen from below, looming in enormity, its topmost ramparts converging in the sky. And so on. For such reasons—for the glamor of the letters—I persevered, despite Miss W's impatience.

As I grew older, the graphic synesthesia faded. My devotion to letters only grew, however; and when I was about eleven, I took up calligraphy. I borrowed library books describing chancery italic, blackletter, and something breezy and chilled called "Gaelic round hand"—each character dismembered on the page, its strokes anatomized, numbered, named. My parents indulged me with trips to the art-supply store for the necessaries: penholders; fat, promising bottles of inks in all colors; and the faintly menacing steel nibs—which, I was gratified to discover, came in left-handed models, with points specially angled. It all came to an end when I botched another teacher's wedding announcement—my first commission, and my last.

My dad's typewriter offered other pleasures. It was an undistinguished Royal, and a portable, which lived in a plastic briefcase all its own. I liked to hammer away at the keys while it sat before me, nestled like some kind of chattering clam in its open case, and fill numberless pages with its loose-limbed, monospace characters. In truth, I found the sharp letter arms swinging in their oblique angles faintly menacing, an unwitting evocation of William S. Burroughs's monstrous, arthropodal Clark Nova—though when

I pushed all the keys I could cover with my two open palms, they crowded rather ridiculously at the platen, less a locust's maw than a mob of rowdy fans lining up at a ticket window. As with calligraphy, I was more interested in making marks than making sense; at the typewriter, I busied myself creating meaningless grids of letters, letters in waves and curves, big letters pieced together out of small.

A few years later, a friend received an electronic typewriter for a birthday. It was a Smith-Corona with a tiny, wet-looking rectangle of liquid crystal topping the keys; in "auto mode," one typed without making marks on paper, watching instead as a parade of alphanumerics piled by in pixelated lockstep. Saved to a memory buried somewhere in the machine's innards, the characters would later tumble and smash their way onto pages of letter-size bond at the touch of a button. A group of us clustered around it when the time for senior-year theses arrived, watching in rapt silence as the thing typed out a fifteen-page term paper with unearthly speed, keys untouched as the daisy wheel rattled and spun.

Already by junior high, however, there had been rumors of computers; one midwinter quarter, a clutch of beige Apple II's took up residence in a disused shop classroom. Their displays filled up with letters in unearthly green, stacked clumsily out of tiny blocks of glow. But these were letters that could do things, make things; they seemed to pick and choose their forces and effects in ways unknown to the letter on the page. They seemed less symbols or servants than companions crowding into the space of the screen, claiming a life of their own from electricity and the black-boxed quiddity of the system.

I summon up this grab bag of biographical oddities to explain why I've turned to a history of writing, and to intuit what hope might be recoverable from that history for writing's fate in the digital age. In my reading for this book, I've looked for glimmers of the same fascination with letters, with script, and with the material of writing that has been a fixture of my imagination from the start. But these glimmers shine beyond the limits of personal obsession: calligraphy, the Palmer Method, the portable typewriter, the Apple II: each indexes a shift in writing as a mode of personal experience. But they are not so much inevitable stages of a teleology as they are moments in the long, churning life of the written word.

In the writing we do—in the writing I do anyway, day in and day out—these modes and materials lie superimposed, one atop the other, mingling and a-jumble. My finger still remembers the ridged callus raised by pencils too-tightly held; the tap-a-tap chant of the typewriter sings subconsciously as I caress the keys of my MacBook Air. These textures of sense and method come together like a palimpsest—an ancient form of recycling, which the Oxford English Dictionary defines as a "writing surface on which the original text has been effaced or partially erased, and then overwritten by another." This practical paean to ancient economy doesn't exhaust the meanings of "palimpsest," however; for as the OED points out, the word also refers, "in extended use," to "a thing likened to such a writing surface, esp. in having been reused or altered while still retaining traces of its earlier form." The OED marshals the words of Thomas De Quincey in support of this definition: *What else than a natural and mighty palimpsest is the human brain?*

BOOKS IN RUNNING BROOKS

A Letter is a joy of Earth —
It is denied the Gods —

—EMILY DICKINSON

See, I have engraved you on the palms of my hands;
your walls are ever before me.

—ISAIAH 49:16, NIV

A letter always arrives at its destination.

—JACQUES LACAN

R eading has existed for hundreds of thousands of years, but writing is a recent invention. The exclamation of a flower in the forest's green expanse; the broken phrase of tracks in the snow; the ragged rhythm that certain species of game birds make when gathering for migratory flight, murder and murmuration—our ancestors' interpretations of these broken melodies were always reading's precursors.

"Find tongues in trees, books in running brooks, sermons in stones," Duke Senior instructs in *As You Like It*, "and good in everything." All the clarity and confusion, all the rapture of reading is found in our pattern-haunted wont.

So while writing is a recent invention, the needs it answers are ancient ones. Its mandate emerged as our ancestors by slow, imperceptible degrees started to turn mere stimuli into the thousand-figured faces of the imaginal world, imbuing them with agency, with identity, with life. The empathetic encounter that takes place in a reader of a novel, in which characters' states of mind leap off the page, has its ancient antecedents in our meaning-pregnant engagement with the natural world. The stages of this transformation were more likely those of an imperceptible blossoming than a disruptive transformation—an evolved and evolving state, revolutionary only in retrospect.

The characters in which this page is set, too, are products of—and in a sense escapees from—evolution; indeed they comprise some of the most complex and highly evolved of all the "endless forms most beautiful and most wonderful" found on the tangled bank Darwin contemplates at the end of *On the Origin of Species*. We do well to remember that letters are born of the natural world; their loops and serifs contain, coiled within them like DNA, the story of their making and remaking: the imprint or inscription of pixel, machine, steel tool, nib, quill, brush, and reed. Like trees, their past lives encircle one another, bound into their matrix down to the very sapling in the heartwood. And in the process of evolutionary change, writing has buried its roots deep within our cultures, our very consciousness. Writing is a meme—a whole flock of them, really—a community of beguiling ideas nesting within one another, for whom the mind (extended, distributed) is the essential ecology. And yet unlike with language—unlike even *reading* of the broad, ineluctably human kind described above—we can get by perfectly well without writing. For tens upon tens of thousands of years, we *did* get by without it—and millions of people do today. Writing can be absent from the brain without causing trauma in a way that cannot be said of language. And yet once rooted there, it will not be excised.

Writing needs us more than we need it. Like chess, neoclassical architecture, and religion, it is a thing that feeds on consciousness, requires the human mind in order to survive and propagate. To describe it this way takes away no grandeur or wonder from the magnificent contingency that is writing; indeed, it's the basis of my celebration. Writing does not have *to be*—and yet it *is*, in a multitude of forms. And it is evolving ever more speedily in minds made fertile with text, image, and imagination. Like Darwin's tangled bank, writing's "elaborately constructed forms, so different from each other, and dependent upon each other in so complex a manner, have all been produced by laws acting around us." Only, in the case of writing, these laws act *through* us, not as dumb or blind agents but as the very work of the human brain.

There is a favored metaphor for writing's tangled skein of overlapping figurations: the palimpsest. The ink and faint imprint of the prior text underlies the new work, preserving a trace of something that had been rubbed out. Like the related genre of poetry called the palinode, in which the poet recants but cannot ever wholly efface some prior opinion, the palimpsest is evidence that there is no true erasure. Some remnant trace will always escape the grasp of the author-eraser. A page of text, however freshly inked, will always be a palimpsest: beneath Roman letters, the Greek; beneath the printed serifs, the Humanist script and the column of Trajan; beneath the marble, the back-and-forth cadences of an ox pulling its plow through Mesopotamian earth. And as the palimpsest of writing reaches back into time, it wills itself forward as well into new forms—which, however they try to erase the old, are committed to bearing their traces.

Freud seized upon a fruitful modern version of the palimpsest in the short essay "A Note Upon the 'Mystic Writing Pad,'" in which he explores the erasable wax tablet to illustrate his idea of the links between perception and memory. Most writing media, he argues, offered imperfect versions of memory: either they are too finite and fixed (the notepad) or too ephemeral (the wax tablet or the slate). The problem is one of storage versus flexibility. "An unlimited receptive capacity and a retention of permanent traces," he writes, "seem to be mutually exclusive properties in the apparatus which we use as substitutes for our memory: either the receptive surface must be renewed or the note must be destroyed." Freud's suggestive example is a toy called the "mystic writing pad," modern examples of which consist of a wax-covered card with a plastic overlay attached at the top edge. Using a stylus, one writes upon the plastic overlay, pressing it into the dark wax below, which shows through as a mark on the translucent plastic. By peeling the overlay from the wax one "erases" these marks, as it were magically: in like fashion do perceptions arrive to the mind, making contact with the substrates of memory and the unconscious; their traces last awhile, until the outer surface is swept clean. Atop it all, a clear layer seeks to protect the fragile ego (I mean the slip of plastic) from permanent damage by limiting the force of impressions intruding from the outside world. And yet a trace always remains—beneath the superficial layers, down in the dark wax, the remembered inscriptions mingle indelibly.

The title of Freud's essay—"A Note Upon the 'Mystic Writing Pad'"—is punning; read wrong, it makes it sound as if he composed his work upon the very *Wunderblock* it describes. Like a message on the mystic pad, Freud's theories have largely been peeled away from our latter-day discourse—and yet they remain impressed into the dark, sticky stuff of the collective unconscious, where they've taken up residence among an uneasy palimpsest of gods, myths, and constellations. The bright lines have faded, but the grooves remain. This pattern is both deeply human and fundamental to life on Earth, which is also palimpsestic: fingers, fins, and prismatic feathers all laid down over primordial symmetries, traces of ancient precellular symbioses, misty fragments of life's first tentative lines.

Of characters themselves, they too begin in inscription: the word derives from the Greek χαρακτηρ (*kharaktếr*), a tool for marking or graving, and the verb χαρακτηιν (*kharaktéin*), to engrave, incise, cut. The first uses of the word "character" in English refer not to letters per se, but to graven marks and symbols of all kinds; it didn't come into use for alphabetic letters until the introduction of printing (and printed letters are derived from carved and cast glyphs, of course). Our sense of character as personality—of character as the graph of an individual's unique qualities—relates to aspects formed from contact with the world and fellow humans: John Stuart Mill writes in *On Liberty* that "a person whose desires and impulses are his own—are the expression of his own nature, *as it has been developed and modified by his own culture*—is said to have a character" (my emphasis). In my neighborhood there is a solitary pine of great age whose trunk takes a detour: twenty feet from the ground, it bends outward in an open parenthesis some five or six feet high before continuing its vertical climb to the canopy. At some point, the tree must have reached a sort of accommodation with some long-lost neighbor's limb, whose trace remains literally alive in its surviving cousin. In the same way do written characters, following their own meter but modified by the world, come into maturity.

When at my rest,
those are those
possessing more.
In a self-
possession...
And what is
Fortune but
Affection and
what is Affection
but the Germ
of the little
Note?
A Letter is a
Joy of Earth —
It is denied
the Gods.

Emily,
with Love

The ancient Indo-European root of "palimpsest" denotes devouring; a "character" is a thing that is cut; "to write," too, derives from an ancient clan of Germanic words for scoring, slicing, and tearing. We're back on Darwin's tangled bank, writing a glory of forms most beautiful and wonderful—but with origins that are red in tooth and claw as well. History is a bloody palimpsest, a record of devourings—of rubbings-out, innumerable and imperfect. And writing systems, after all, are infamously imperfect, full of holes and lacunae that both leave us bereft and spur further evolution.

But a measure of writing's power also springs from its limits. "A letter is a joy of Earth," Emily Dickinson writes; "It is denied the Gods"—for omniscience would make writing unnecessary, destroying its pleasure and surprise. The gods are irretrievably beyond letter writing; for them there is no anticipation, no wondering about a letter's (or a line's, or a word's) reception or interpretation. Dickinson's brief poem concerns what might be called epistolary erotics, the pleasures of correspondence: its rhythms of composition and delivery, the intensity of expression and the swirl of anticipation. A letter writer of intensity and passion, Dickinson was intimate with these

FACING PAGE: The "poem" by Emily Dickinson in my epigraph made its first appearance as a phrase in private correspondence. Dickinson favored the phrase; it appears in no fewer than three letters, as revealed in the online Emily Dickinson Archive. It was subsequently edited into published poems, posthumously, by Mabel Loomis Todd. Most of Dickinson's poems—some eight hundred in all—were found posthumously in the form of small gatherings of folded paper, often stitched and bound with thread, called "fascicles." Whether the ordering of their foldings and stitchings reflects mere chronology or a higher editorial order has been a subject of scholarly dispute since these letter-like packets were discovered—and yet crucially, it's apparent from the intensity of the handwriting and the meticulousness of their construction that Dickinson herself was the one to whom the delicious treasure was given to discover the poet, letter by letter, folding and unfolding in time.

joys. And what she says about the epistle holds true for written characters—and doubly so for Dickinson herself, who unspooled her poems in cursive and carefully stitched them into the little booklet bundles scholars call fascicles. Each wide, looping glyph is a missive and an essay, a testament, a trial. To an extent nearly unmatched, Dickinson used writing to compose her life; in a very real sense, hers was a *body* of work—a body made of writing, a composite avatar of poetry and letters flowered out in fascicles. Socrates had faulted letters for their quietude and seeming lack of independent life; for Dickinson, these faults were the powers through which she both concealed and extended herself. Letters are for bridging gaps; misunderstood, they stand like piers of intention at the edge of meaninglessness, the disappointed bridges of Joyce's Stephen Dedalus; like docks and jetties, letters seem to want to connect.

But these messages impose burdens as well. "Missive," after all, shares a root with "mission." Letters not only go on missions from writer to reader, they impose them as well. The magisterium of writing turns composition and comprehension into labor, vocation, even profession. They cannot act alone, the letters; they require putting together and pulling apart.

If Dickinson's plural divinity find writing's needs and pleasures alien, it is God with a capital *G* who would seem most estranged from the scribal burdens; for His solitude, like His knowledge and His power, is absolute. With whom could the omnipotent epistolate, after all? God is a creator, not a communicator. And yet in the Bible, *contra* Dickinson, Yahweh is a writer—and a frustrated author to boot, His correspondents being the constrained beings of His own creation. Only when His tablets are smitten and lost, it seems, do His characters find their way, palimpsest-wise, into the consciences of His creatures, who still ignore the import of the grand text of creation itself, forever rewritten around them and for them. Thus Isaiah 49:16, "Behold I have graven thee upon the palms of my hands"—Yahweh reduced, like a child suitor, to scrawling His love for humankind in the palm of His hand.

For mortals, too, the inscriptions are never certain; with writing there is always the uncertainty of reception, the mystery of the reader. Who is the reader—and who else is reading? Socrates will condemn this mysterious, message-in-a-bottle quality of writing; but like Emily Dickinson, we can learn to embrace these mysteries as well. An implacable corollary of Dickinson's epistolary theology: the fallibility of letters is only a fiction of time. The gods see them written to the very last *finis,* to an end in which their purposes will be fulfilled, their story revealed. "A letter always reaches its destination," wrote Jacques Lacan, concluding his discussion of Poe's story "The Purloined Letter," in which a letter stolen by a blackmailing government minister is found hidden in plain sight. With Lacan, we might agree that even the misdirected message finds, in its unintended recipients, its mission; only when there are no more readers left to be discovered will the words have exhausted their possibilities. It's as if letters have the need to be read, to find their way into the minds their forebears prepared for them—and to prepare those minds for future letters as well. Proliferating, fascinating, fixing, and transforming: these qualities are bound up in what Lacan calls the urge of the letter.

And yet for all its beauty, for all its willing proliferation, transformation, and abundance, writing is hard. It submits us to a painful tuition; it exacts a price. It's fair to ask: what does writing want? Writing presents us with enormous, nearly insurmountable cognitive hurdles—so much about it resists the easy transmission of thought and sensibility made possible by half a million of years of human evolution. We evolved to communicate face-to-face and side by side; gesture accompanies word like cleaner fishes clinging to the body of a shark. The flicker of eyelids, the rhythm of the breath, even the odor and heat of the body, contribute to the conversation. Writing does more than simply strip all this away; it presents the reader with a new set of challenges: decoding and computation, assembly and algorithm. When schoolchildren struggle to learn the craft of the personal essay or the short story, they're addressing the same questions faced by the scribes of ancient Sumer who turned the rude numeracy of gouges in clay into a net for catching language. Pushing arithmetic scrawl beyond the hash mark entailed a leap into symbolic life, into games of metaphor and this-for-that. Into poetry. And what did the ancient scribes have to draw from but their own lives as readers-already, as watching children glimpsing monsters in the cedars and gods in the clouds?

"When I've taught writing," Richard Sennett writes in *The Craftsman*,

> I've asked my students to rewrite the printed instructions that accompany new software. Perfectly accurate, these nefarious publications are often unintelligible. They take dead denotation to an extreme. Not only do engineer-writers leave out "dumb things" that "everyone knows"; they repress simile, metaphor, and adverbial color. The act of unpacking what's buried in the vault of tacit knowledge can make use of these imaginative tools. By invoking the signals birds send by singing or bees by dancing, the person rewriting software instructions can make comprehensible what hypertext does and how economically it should be used.

Of course, writing *is* a craft—and like any craft it must be learned, and to do so one must submit to a discipline that takes place, not in the world of words and images but in the body. The writing teacher can only make use of writing itself to a limited extent; she must resort in the end to somatic realities that reside outside written language. Cast back to schooldays: the hunched posture, the cramped hands, the tongue clamped between the teeth—all indicating the extent to which gesture, posture, and the callisthenic rigors of practice go where written instructions do not. Writing is not learned from written instruction alone; it's a craft of the body, learned corporally—and alas, as novice scribes have attested since Mesopotamian days, one often accompanied by corporal punishment. A contemporary handwriting curriculum calls itself "Handwriting Without Tears"—a noble effort to rid the learning of writing of its wonted discomfort and shame.

In time, those discomforts are tempered; the gestures and postures are internalized, and writing becomes a habit, a reflex, an impulse. This remarkable—and remarkably simple—capacity for writing to become a symbiont of the consciousness, for a craft so sophisticated and cognitively demanding to knit itself securely into our quotidian ways—is as responsible as its great utility for the ineluctable role it plays in modern life. Despite massive technological changes in the media of writing, mere handwriting remains an impulse for even the computationally sophisticated, as the many-petaled blossom of adhesive notes affixed to so many computer monitors attests. Even in a networked age, if handwriting didn't exist, we'd have to invent it.

Such notes typically lack the elegance associated with historic handwriting—and yet traces of the ideal letters live within the most tortured scrawl. Writing confers a utopian belief in what I might like to call *eugraphy*—the formation of true letters (beguiling, eternal, unattainable). We always arrive to writing as beginners in the midst of experts, finding our way by dint of prior written documents, which both inspire and oppress our apprentice efforts.

I call writing's influence on human experience by the name of *mag-isterium*. A word first used to denominate the teaching authority of the Church in theological matters, "magisterium" was also used by Stephen Jay Gould to name the complementary intellectual provinces of Science and Religion. The magisterium of writing is far from the oldest magisterium, not nearly so venerable as music or mythology. But it's one that, for its historical novelty, is deeply interwoven in the individual minds and collective consciousness of we who read and write—so profoundly and intimately reorganiz-ing the literate psyche that the manner in which it wields its power is all but invisible to us. By way of its cognitive charisma, palimpses-tic tracery, and harsh discipline, writing purchases its enduring life in human minds. Perhaps only music and religion are as capable of writing's trick of turning every challenge into an opportunity to extend its magisterium. Throughout its history, writing has con-served and innovated, maintained its ancient ways while extending them into new media and modes. While some immensely import-ant writing forms have died entirely as active systems—cuneiform, Mycenaean Linear A, the glyphs of the Mayans—throughout most of its history writing has developed by incorporating and sup-porting its predecessor forms. A great instance of this comes with the emergence of movable type in the fifteenth century: printing would seem to sound the death knell for manuscript writing, and yet some of the first printed books were the handwriting manuals that made their first appearance in Italy in the first decades of the sixteenth century. Early type designers such as Ludovico Vicen-tino degli Arrighi and Giambattista Palatino were also masters of calligraphy who taught writing and adapted its techniques to the printed page. In their published manuals they disclosed techniques not only for forming letters but for formulating inks and main-taining proper posture, for cutting quills and selecting papers—

and for relating the practice of the pen to the values of humanism. The printmaking methods of intaglio etching and engraving gave calligraphy a life in print in ways that outstripped the ancient practice of woodblock printing—and allowed handwriting techniques to be disseminated to much wider circles than had been thought possible, much less desirable, in the Middle Ages. While the writing masters often extolled the virtues of hands that followed the natural flow of the pen, engravers had a harder time, forcing flowing calligraphy out of the inflexible media of metals and acids, inscribing the fluid hands of the author in reverse, re-creating the fat downstrokes of quills with an ever more specialized armament of burins and other tools. The forms of cast type themselves were based in the shapes of letters rendered by the pen; from the emergence of movable type into the nineteenth century, changes in the technologies of handwriting inspired advances in the engraver's art. Far from eliminating handwriting, print made it possible for calligraphy to develop a space of its own in lettered culture. The printed book cast a long shadow, but handwriting still bloomed within it, taking on new authority, mystery, and intimacy.

Of course, print and manuscript never were in conflict, really; the two practices spring from a single vine. Among the letter's qualities is the urge to proliferate—to radiate and evolve—to exploit the contingencies of history, culture, and materials means to transform itself. We don't *need* writing to do this, but for its growth and progress, writing needs *us*. In many times and places, humans have been content to pass along their writing techniques from generation to generation without the development of new forms. Conservative cultures may hold the pen at arm's length, so to speak, allowing writing only a measured infiltration into art, religion, and daily life. But where it finds an open border, a transitional zone—perhaps at a time of cultural conflict, or religious efflorescence, or in the midst of productively roiling economic change—writing finds its opening, cleaving off new forms and species. And as new forms appear, the old ones shift and adapt to fill new niches. The word "manuscript" does not even appear in English until the impact of the press was felt upon every facet of public life.

I began by saying that reading is older than writing. Although mythology imagines it as a gift from the gods, it emerges in stages: the fickle evolution of *Homo scribens*, the writing ape, an unfolding nature that takes a shape all its own—the shape of history. From its simple origins writing has been proliferating, increasing its powers, enrobing its rituals in sanctity, science, and story. And letter by letter, writing extends its powers over ever more far-flung domains.

ORIGINS AND NATURE

The Urge of the Letter

Writing is both self-evident and elusive—like music, it's easy to recognize but difficult to explain. The tradition in the West has been to define writing in evolutionary terms, tracing a progressive line from the pictograms and mnemonic hash marks of Mesopotamian cuneiform through complex ideogrammic systems like Chinese and Egyptian hieroglyphics, to the austere, analytic simplicity of the roman alphabet with its twenty-six precisely modulated consonants and vowels.

Of course, it's never so simple; the alphabet-as-ideal differs markedly from the alphabet-in-practice. For one thing, there isn't only *one* alphabet: the sets of characters we call "uppercase" and "lowercase" (thanks to the inventions of print) actually constitute *two* separate, intertwined alphabets; the roman and the italic are two more subspecies within the genus *Alphabet*, cousins to the Greek and Etruscan letters, to the Hebrew, the Persian, and the Dravidian all issuing from the same Phoenician stock, each writing stories of its own. Second, all of the punctuation and diacritical marks that indicate pronunciation, rhythm, and emphasis—none of which are alphabetic—are also writing. Inscribed signs have cleaved from language to serve as enumeration and musical notation, as shorthand, corporate logos, signatures, graffiti tags, and logico-mechanical parts in computational machines. These ancillary and enhancing systems, these add-ons and also-rans, have histories of their own, offering a reminder of the bewildering diversity of marks and makings that are entangled with language.

The qualities that separate humanity from the other animals—qualities upon which the most magnificently developed aspects of civilization are founded—are also so basic to our species that they can properly be called instinctive. I mean memory, and the longing for it—the impatience to make a mark, to see one's being figured in time; I mean language, its meaning-making drive, which most often (but not always) takes the form of oral speech; the everywhere-emergent urge to name and to describe but also to promise, to vow, to lie, and to tell stories; the impulse to see pattern for pattern, to transpose color into music, growth into movement, event into tale, speech into line. Before the emergence of a particular group of letters, before all the sets of hieroglyphics and pictograms and syllabaries, writing is contrived of a deeper-foundationed alphabet: the visible provinces of the electromagnetic spectrum; the neural reflexes that have our eyes follow flickering movements, giving rise to the perception of figure and ground; and the tragic sensation of time's passage, which makes speech and all of life into line and punctuation.

So the great chain of alphabetical evolution collapses in a welter of characters, glyphs, and symbols mingling in friendly, familial, and even erotic enthusiasms of conversant meaning. There are modes, moods, and qualities running through this welter, not only segmenting and differentiating but affiliating, resonating, combining, rhyming. Even among the characters with which any literate English-speaker is familiar, these modes act like musical scales or keys to give particular themes or tempers to our signification. Take numerals: Most of us have little difficulty counting by twos, threes, or fives, or even backward starting anywhere in the set of real numbers, often without a conscious sense of arithmetic or calculation. And yet try doing the same with another series of symbols that take a definite order: the alphabet. Right now, try to say the alphabet backward. Try writing it backward, if you have a pencil handy. Unless you're practiced at it, or a savant, it's impossible to do this without enormous mnemonic exertion.* It's as if the alphabet has a *grain*, like the bark of a tree or a shark's skin; it's only smooth when you rub it in the right direction. Number, at least in the first instance, seems bidirectional, ambidextrous. What do such modes or moods reveal about our systems of meaning—something about our cognitive makeup, or about kinds and categories of meaning; or do they tell us about the practices and habits with which we condition ourselves in the learning process? Of course it is all these things—nature, nurture, and the patient teachings of the signs.

---

* I was impressed from the start with my wife's capacity to recite the alphabet backward. She's a mathematician and computer programmer, and I assumed that it was further evidence of her prodigious powers of mental calculation. Jealous of her talent, I practiced the backward alphabet assiduously for a couple of weeks, only making progress once I had found a way to set it to the Mozartean melody most of us use to learn the alphabet in the first place. The setting is elusive, of course, because our names for the letters aren't metrically symmetrical; the trouble comes in around the letter *F*. Finally I nailed it down from *Z* to *A*, reciting it to Rebekah with pride. She then admitted that her ability to go through the alphabet in reverse was not preternatural but learned: she and her sister had worked out the alphabet song in reverse themselves when they were children.

I am willing to bet that the answer, ultimately, involves all of these areas—depending on one's perspective it appears a gathering of cognitive, social, and cultural energies. But preeminently the secret of writing lies in the very possibility of synthesis. For a letter, after all, can also be a number (if I've said it once, I hasten to point out, I've said it M times). Our very perception that one thing can stand for another—metaphor, the world's uncanny habit of speaking to itself through us—permits an unlimited process of making and extending meanings. The palette for those signs, however, comes to us via the constrained, peculiar spectrum of our senses: the sights, sounds, smells, tastes, and textures that our natural history bequeaths us. Human writing embodies human particularities; dolphin writing or squid writing would work in very different ways (the squid's ink notwithstanding). This may seem a trivial or self-evident observation, but it determines writing's qualities and constraints in forcible ways.

God's tablets brought down from Mount Sinai, angelic messages, and the esoteric symbols of alchemical essences—though they are missives from transcendent realms—all come to us as *human* documents. And late in the history of writing, when we begin to extend the work of writing to the digital realm, we find that the fluid character of letters, shaped by human hands, finds affinities with the sensory and cognitive habits of machines.

No Words but in Things

Classical writing theory began with memory, with the impulse to preserve the percussive and ephemeral acts and things of oral speech. Of course, there is no simple, direct system of correspondences between oral and visual signs; language changes, writing changes, and the skein of correspondences between the two grows ever more tangled. But this growing complexity, which might have been an obstacle to the emergence of writing, becomes part of the power (and pleasure) even of simple writing systems. In other words, writing, in addition to being a means of recording and expressing, is also a medium of play. By devising a simple writing system, perhaps I can make my meaning clear. We'll start as many of our ancestors did, with pictures:

I'm trying to say, "I see you"; I've cast about for handy symbols to represent each word/idea in the statement, settling on stick figures for people (the problems with this approach are obvious; I'll return to them shortly). For the verb, another picture, albeit one that works in a slightly different way from the first: a metonym, it uses a part or particle to suggest the whole, and—given our deep-ingrained responsiveness to the human eye—this one would seem a fairly efficient choice.

Already, of course, we've been forced to do a little bit of analytic work, at least to suggest the shape of a structured set of symbols based on things that have to do with seeing. The stick figures, however, represent a problem of a different order. Even before addressing the grammatical challenge of distinguishing subject from object, we face the more basic problem of distinguishing what is what. Their identicality produces ambiguity, which acts like a bug in the software, forcing the whole syntactical program to shut down. The group of symbols doesn't "read" as a statement but as a mere association. We can't tell what's going on. Does one person share an eye with another? Are they two believers in some cult of the Great Eye? Is it in fact an eye at all—could it be a well, or maybe a big piece of fruit, or a basketball balanced on a surfboard?

My first attempt has turned out rather badly. What to do? Ambiguity notwithstanding, I'd suggest that the eye glyph works pretty well; it's the people that need help. We could begin by devising some sort of inflection, some accents or diacritics that could help us distinguish the actors in the play. Already with this notion, we're moving beyond the mimetic and into the semiographic, emphasizing the ostensive, symbol-making possibilities of the graphic in parity with the pictorial. Perhaps an arrow pointing toward the figure for "I," and one pointing away for "you," would do—or better, a figure indicating itself for the first person, and one pointing toward our nascent reader for the second:

Of course, we'll have to agree to the convention, especially to the understanding that the "I want you" figure means the word "you," and not any particular reader. By doing so, we're pushing our system further away from the simple rebus pictography we started out with, into a realm that's more removed from oral speech, and more analytic, more variable, and supple. But the trade-off is a loss of immediacy and universal translatability—ideals that have haunted writing from the very start.

But there's another route to a solution, one that plays with the strange flavors of oral speech and graphic possibility. Remembering the strangely echolalic nature of words, we cast about for homonyms and tender some transpositions:

We've lost the metonymic, part-for-whole immediacy of our verb's sign. We're playing quite specifically with the basic stuff of language—a particular language, in fact: English, with all its special sounds and effects. In tying our signs to one oral language, we've gained a bit of comedy (admittedly of a low sort); in a kind of metaphysical drama, meanwhile, we've also reenacted humankind's expulsion from the Garden, the fall of the Tower of Babel (or *Baah*-bel, perhaps?), and the confusion of the tongues.

From the great stream of history that flows out of the once-fertile region between the Tigris and the Euphrates, building from the incised clay of cuneiform into all coves and harbors of the alphabet; to the equally strong current rising out of China to fill the East; writing systems seem to leap up fully formed to flood the tablet, the stone, the leaf with words. And yet like a flood, writing expands a language by stealing into it: disciplining and ordering it, noting its nakedness and making it visible. And as it clothes language, writing hides its own traces, leaving metaphysical lacunae that have haunted thinkers about writing for ages.

But this pictographic play doesn't begin to approach the complexity of writing's emergence. Minimally, writing is a visual encoding of language; in practice, ways of writing transcend oral speech. Written symbols can stand for musical tones or rhythms, mathematical operations, or denominations of currency, to name a very few possibilities. Our system could make more extensive use of semiographic signs—accents and marks to distinguish cognitive tones and colors, to specify and intensify. Such sigils featured in early writing systems like cuneiform and the systems that arose from Egyptian hieroglyphs, to differentiate homophonic words; they return in the forms of tags and character encodings that allow us to index electronic texts for searching and manipulating them in meaningful ways. In the present case, we could agree to conventions that tell us when the "eye" letter is referring to the organ of vision or to its first-person-singular homophone. Unlike our tentative finger-jab in this direction with the stick figures above, our semiographic intensifier will be abstract and explicitly arbitrary—perhaps a simple horizontal line across the top will do.

I've given the ewe the same treatment, thus making it a "you." And I've thrown another surprise into the bargain, adding a new symbol to stand for a different verb. I suspect you've managed to read the statement without difficulty, as it expresses itself with a commonly accepted semiotic marker for romance/eros/*cupiditas*/Valentine's Day. And now, dear reader—for such you have become—my writing system can express my sentiments, engendered by your patient and thoughtful consideration.

One of writing's great achievements is that, like the languages it encodes or completes or parasitizes, it manages to be extensible: by means both cognitive and social, it enlarges itself to address novel states of affairs. It proceeds with this magic by means that are native to human minds—analogy, metaphor, mimesis, and classification, to name a few. It also exploits (and transforms) circuits in our brains to make itself at home there. You may not be able to say the alphabet backward, but msot poelpe cna raed wirtetn smatetetns taht srcmalbe teh ltetres wtiihn wrdos—a powerful example of writing's powers of cognitive domestication. Writing teaches our brains to do all kinds of somersaults and tricks.

Writing also exhibits the uncanny property of disembodiment; a written sign can stand and deliver its message ad infinitum, regardless of its author's fate. Haunting and uncanny, writing made Socrates uncomfortable; its seemingly supernatural durability also unsettled Jesus, whose followers would richly and tortuously figure this ambivalence in letters. This immortal tendency of writing entranced and troubled the kings of Mesopotamia with its capacity both to underline and to undermine royal authority: inscribed in stone, recorded on tablets, their victories were both preserved and subject to revision.

According to an old understanding of human nature that remains quite popular, writing marks a divide between savagery and civilization. Before its advent, men and women toiled in witless fear, crisscrossing featureless landscapes without the knowledge and wisdom of their ancestors to guide them, losing track of the generations in the abyss of myth and forgetting. To such humans, the past was the home of an oblivion as deadly as the future. In place of literature, they chanted mind-numbing verses; lacking history, they cowered in fear of primordial fantasies. In place of knowledge there was the capricious comprehensiveness of myth; rather than the stable mandate of law, the tyranny of present needs. By this understanding, writing bestows historical consciousness and stable individual identity, government and archives, science and study, the past and the future. Of all the capacities that bind and blur savagery and civilization, writing would seem to draw a bright line between them.

Yet perhaps the line is not so bright. For although we take writing to be the sine qua non of history—the very medium in which the past comes into sharp focus and our relation to it becomes measurable—the stories of its origins are often the subject of myth. To a degree unlike some of the other lumber of civilization—law, science, mathematics, and literature, all of which depend upon it—writing is rooted in a mythological cosmos of archetypes and associations, homeopathy and homology, magic and mystery.

Of course, an invention as complex and essentially unfinished as writing must have difficult-to-trace roots, branching and fine-fibered. And like many mythical creatures, writing is faced with the paradox of having to erupt or evolve or birth itself out of a collocation of things that aren't writing at all. This is not only a logical conundrum, but the very problem of existence queried in a thousand ways by mythology—a way of making and taking stock of meaning in the world that writing, historically, fundamentally disrupts (but never eradicates). It's also the compelling mystery figured by the theory of natural selection. But the challenge of writing's history is more deeply inscribed than this. For there is among those who read and write the sense that written characters exist apart from time, that they partake of the ineffable and the ideal. "Letters are things, not pictures of things," said type designer Eric Gill, echoing the intuition of the kabbalists. Regardless of the writing system or the medium in which they are inscribed, glyphs have qualities that lend themselves quite readily to reinscription, proliferation, and transmediation. And thus as oral cultures wink out one by one, traces of some remain in writing—worked into the textual contraptions we call literature—their preservation ensured by the medium of their undoing.

Signs and Wonders

We see the search for writing's power everywhere in mythology. Take the *Kalevala*, the Finnish national epic. Its hero, Väinämöinen, wise singer of the labyrinthine taiga and the mist-shrouded islands of the White Sea, wished to build himself a boat. Out beyond the trees and seeping bogs, he knew, the secrets and powers of the world itself swirled, and he wished to seek them out. His helper, young Sampsa Pellervöinen, had already spoken to the trees to ask for lumber, had found that oak would answer where ash and fir demurred. And Väinämöinen took up the wood and did what any eternal bard would do: he sang to it.

> *Väinämöinen, old and skilful,*
> *The eternal wonder-worker,*
> *Builds his vessel with enchantment,*
> *Builds his boat by art of magic,*
> *From the timber of the oak-tree,*
> *From its posts, and planks, and flooring.*
> *Sings a song, and joins the frame-work;*
> *Sings a second, sets the siding;*
> *Sings a third time, sets the row-locks;*
> *Fashions oars, and ribs, and rudder,*
> *Joins the sides and ribs together.*

At first, the hero's magic is entirely oral: the glamor of the singer. But the boat is not yet made ready; Väinämöinen realizes that he lacks the "three words of master magic" that will join the hand-rails, smooth the stern, and shape the prow.

Where to find these words of magic,
Find the lost-words of the Master:
"From the brains of countless swallows,
From the heads of swans in dying,
From the plumage of the gray-duck?"
For these words the hero searches,
Kills of swans a goodly number,
Kills a flock of fattened gray-duck,
Kills of swallows countless numbers,
Cannot find the words of magic,
Not the lost-words of the Master.
Väinämöinen, wisdom-singer,
Still reflected and debated:
"I perchance may find the lost-words
On the tongue of summer-reindeer,
In the mouth of the white squirrel."

Amidst the avatars of the natural world, these words of power preexist as things. But the epic of Väinämöinen makes no particular mention of written signs; for their specific emergence in old tales, we can look west, to the haunts of the Norse gods, and to shape-shifting Odin, who sought the wisdom that would give him power throughout the nine realms of existence. It was a boon that only sacrifice could grant; and Odin so desired this power that he scourged himself and hung gibbeted upon the world-tree, Yggdrasil the ash:

I know that I hung, on a wind-rocked tree,
nine whole nights, with a spear wounded,
and to Odin offered, myself to myself;
on that tree, of which no one knows
from which root it springs.

Uncared-for, abandoned, Odin hung in misery, until wisdom revealed itself in the form of the runes hidden among the roots—

Bread no one gave me, nor a horn of drink,
downward I peered, to runes applied myself,
wailing learnt them, then fell down hence.

These runes, like the poetry that can be made from them, were not Odin's alone; they are the gift of his sacrifice to men and the gods.

Runes thou wilt find, and explained characters,
very large characters, very potent characters,
which the great speaker depicted,
and the high powers formed,
and the power's prince graved . . .

Knowest thou how to grave them?
Knowest thou how to expound them?
Knowest thou how to depict them?

The myth-inspiring glamor of letters isn't a power restricted to their earliest phases; throughout writing's career, people have been looking at the letters they inscribe and seeing signs, wonders, and origins. The characters of the alphabet were adapted by their Semitic-speaking creators from a combination of cursive cuneiform figures and Egyptian hieroglyphs that had come to stand for syllables in polyglot ancient Western Asia; modern archaeologists have associated the glyphs of the proto-Canaanite alphabet, which coalesced about 1700 BCE, with a putative mnemonic tale—a story about an ox, a house, and a plow—now lost, which gave the alphabet its order. It's a marvelous story, and—like most marvelous stories—no one knows if it's true. Even the science-molding scholars of the nineteenth century, smitten with the rediscovered marvels of cuneiform, began telling just-so stories in which they dreamed from the scratched, angular rudiments of Mesopotamian scripts tales of alphabets reduced from spells and stories, an ox in the Aleph, a house in Beth.

In the sixteenth century, English astronomer, alchemist, and mystic John Dee claimed to have discovered the language of the angels, the primordial pre-Babel tongue from which human language is descended, transmitted to him in a writing system of enigmatic runes and glyphs. Dee's angelic language held more in common with the glossolalia of ecstatic Christianity than early writing systems, but this didn't keep his wonders and fancies from finding an audience—Dee's Enochian alphabet exists today in several digital fonts.

Perhaps the most evocative of writing's origin stories thrives not because of its mystical glamor but for its poetic expression of the fickle and troubling powers writing carries right down to our own time. Socrates, who will leave no words written in his own hand, calls into question not only the utility of writing but its safety. Discoursing with Phaedrus on the nature of love and the trouble caused by persuasive words while walking the road outside Athens, Socrates tells the story of Thoth, the Egyptian god of messengers and calculators, who took the form of the ibis, a water bird that frequents the muddy, papyrus-laden banks of the Nile.

Thoth was keen and curious, a handy inventor of tools, which included arithmetic and astronomy as well as dice. But of all his inventions he was happiest with letters, the rudiments of writing. Proudly he shows them to Thamus, the god-king of Egypt. *Letters*, said Thoth, *will make the Egyptians wiser and give them better memories; it is an elixir both for the memory and for the wit.* But Thamus in his wisdom is skeptical. *You who are the father of letters,* he continued, *have been led to attribute to them a quality which they cannot have; for this discovery of yours will create forgetfulness in the learners' souls, because they will not use their memories; they will trust to the external written characters and not remember of themselves. The elixir which you have discovered is an aid not to memory but to reminiscence, and you give your disciples not truth but only the semblance of truth; they will be hearers of many things and will have learned nothing; they will appear to be omniscient and will generally know nothing; they will be tiresome company, having the show of wisdom without the reality.*

Comparing word work to farming, Socrates tells Phaedrus that writing sequesters ideas in a garden of letters—beautiful, fascinating, but walled off from the soul. He admonishes Phaedrus that it may be noble to sow in the garden of letters, but *nobler far is the serious pursuit of the dialectician, who, finding a congenial soul, by the help of science sows and plants therein words which are able to help themselves and him who planted them.*

Far nobler, certainly, Phaedrus agrees.

The relationship to writing evinced by Socrates—as well as his amanuensis, poet, and explainer, Plato—is ambivalent and complicated. Especially when considering the role of writing in creating and sustaining power and authority, a subject this book takes up in a later chapter, Plato's and Socrates's different perspectives on writing, poetry, and learning clash and combine in ways that would prove unsettling and productive for Western thought. But here, in his dialogue with Phaedrus, we have Socrates's intuition that writing emerges as a rupture—that it breaks a healthy order reaching back to the roots of humankind. This skepticism about writing—arising from the oral world of mythology—will itself prove perennially influential.

It's tempting to look for space between the lines of myth and text, between nature and culture, the imaginal worlds of ancient strivings—to put the disparate energies of these mythical accounts of writing origins into dialogue. Here I introduce another one of writing's mythical personae, a cousin to the company of gods and heroes whose inventiveness and industry the stories have credited. Kalamos was the son of Maiandros, a god who took the form of the Meander River in Asia Minor. He fell in love with another youth, Karpos, the child of a nymph and the West Wind. In a riparian rage, Kalamos's father drowned Karpos—the two youths were in the midst of a swimming race, but we're left to wonder whether the river god disapproved of their intimacy—and Kalamos, in his despair, drowned himself. At the moment of his death he becomes the river reed. In the guise of Nilotic papyrus, perhaps, he is the medium by which Egyptian hieroglyphs leap from stone into circulation. But he also gives his name to the writing implements made by people across the ancient world from reed and stem: Sanskrit *kalama*, *calamus* in Latin, in Arabic *qalam*. By the nonverbal mimesis that is prior to words, Kalamos also names the quill of the feather.

But all that comes after the tale I want to tell—a syncretic, enjambed mishmash of a riff, a thought experiment in mythic key: Sunstruck and warm, grieving and green, the youth lay in the river where the mud gives way to water. He sighed, and ripples wrote their way across the long surface of the stream, as he runs in his mind over the long legend of the days and nights of his family—

of his father, who was the river himself, and of the titans and nymphs and spirits of their lineage. And of his love who was fleet as the wind, but no swimmer. The youth occupies himself this way through the blinking of days and floods and seasons and civilizations, down the half-life of his grief, a long-ebbing energy in search of an entelechy. Amidst this musing on the strange past, this rhyming and reasoning and sighing, he spies a curious figure—black and white and all business, his dark head sharpening to a long, hooked beak—dipping along the muddy bank.

"Dear Kalamos," says the beaked fellow. "Still rustling with discontent?"

"Ah, Thoth," Kalamos replies, wind passing through nodding corn. "If only you knew what I have known. Such restless beauty, and the hateful implacability of fate. The very stuff of life and the universe is fickle and inconstant. . . ."

"Yes, quite," says Thoth, rearranging the feathers of a glossy white wing. "I find that I have so little time to trouble myself with such things, however."

"Dear bird," says the youth, "whatever else is there to trouble over?"

"Business!" croaks Thoth. "The balance of Good and Evil, the infinitely variable weights of souls, the entire catalogue of random events and associations that constitute the universe!"

"Ah yes," Kalamos sighs. "But then you are Ra's vice-regent. The very mouthpiece of divinity itself."

"Precisely," Thoth says. "And permit me to take your mind off your troubles by offering for contemplation an invention I'm working on, something to ease the burden of my endless, thankless vocation."

"It sounds quite useful," Kalamos replies. "What is it?"

Thoth's head swivels, his beak describing a suspicious arc as he checks for spies and eavesdroppers in the reeds. "It's—a system," he hisses conspiratorially.

"Mmm, a system," Kalamos muses. "Well, there are plenty of those already. The sun rises and sets; the stars wheel about the pole; even the weather is a system. Why does the cosmos need another?"

"It's not for the cosmos; it's for me," Thoth clacks, bounding up and down on bending legs. "I have so much to keep track of—so many ideas, so many things!"

"That's what *this* is for," Kalamos says, reaching over and tapping Thoth on the head. "So, in any case, what's your idea?"

"I got it walking along this river just now," Thoth replies. "I'm stumping along, trying to keep track of the souls I have to judge, and all of Ra's pronouncements and plans, my feet sinking into the mud with each step—with each step a new concern, a fresh fact, an emerging edict. And I'm looking at my footprints in the mud, each one a perfect imprint of my sole. . . ."

"They *are* fetching," Kalamos remarks, admiring the long line of Thoth's tracks tracing the ripples at river's edge.

"And I thought, 'A thought for each step. An idea for each trace. Each footprint represents an idea!'"

"A remarkable notion. But how to keep track of which idea formed with which footprint?"

It's Thoth's turn to tap his head, flourishing the fan of one wing. "Memory, my grief-stricken reed," he replies. "Memory is the thing."

"So . . . you picture in your mind the track you made in the sand at the moment you were thinking the idea you wish to remember."

"Precisely! So, just now I was thinking of this new system of mine, and so there it is: the track that signifies this very system."

"Quite effective! Only . . . only it looks like almost all of the other tracks, more or less."

"Yes. . . ."

"Even the ways it differs aren't all that different from track to track."

"Yes. . . ."

"So. What will you do when you wish to remember the ideas you've had, but in a different order?"

Thoth can withdraw into himself at such moments, wings sealing to form a smooth shield, unruffled in the inscrutability of his wading-bird nature. After a long while he says, "I do see a whole set of new problems in light of this. But there is a solution: Make each track slightly different! Each track, tied as it is to a unique idea, becomes unique in itself! Like so—"

And Thoth staggers off along the riverbank, varying his gait according to the ideas passing through his mind. Kalamos watches awhile bemusedly. The bird god's japes do take his mind off his world-consuming grief. But, he supposes, it's greater solace to be of service. And so he arises next to the capering ibis and, bending in the river breeze, offers himself to the bird as a simple tool. "Try making your varied tracks with this instrument instead of your toes," he remarks, "and so regain your regal composure."

Like the wearingly systematic ibis, humans strive to put rough-hewn pieces of the world together in useful combinations—a process which, before writing's advent, first took form as myth. And mythology, as the late anthropologist Claude Lévi-Strauss strove to show, is a kind of rigor by other means. To say that writing's invention is the stuff of myth is *not* to say that it arises out of a superstitious morass, but that its emergence is in and of the world, a natural phenomenon like all that myth enfolds and explains, from storms to love and war. Words are the stuff we humans conjure with. Like Thoth and Väinämöinen, we seek to build things with words; like Kalamos and Odin, we suffer to conjure their power and salving splendor. This cobbling together of disparate notions and things is what Lévi-Strauss famously called *bricolage*, taken from the Gallic image of the *bricoleur*, who is something of a handyman, something of a hobbyist—and something (it must be said) of a caveman, too. It's an image that attracted and provoked thinkers well beyond the precinct of anthropology in which Lévi-Strauss's work ostensibly lives. It's a handy metaphor, a brilliant example of the spirit it seeks to pinpoint, and a marvelous demonstration of Lévi-Strauss's own tendency to mythmaking (for *bricolage* itself, in the end, is but a myth).

"The 'bricoleur,'" we are told, "is adept at performing a large number of diverse tasks . . . the rules of his game are always to make do with 'whatever is at hand.' . . . He interrogates all the heterogeneous objects of which his treasury is composed . . . he remains within the constraints imposed by a particular state of civilization." But here's where the mystery arises, for the bricoleur at once seems not only the constrained, but the constrainer—the force that cobbles together the stuff of culture and the wily, erstwhile jobber who works within it—the author of the myth and its singer. And while the latter is locatable as an individual human being, the former would seem lost in deep time. In the midst of this science of signs, the bricoleur is a kind of intellectual Zelig, a holy ghost, a floating signifier who is also the floating signified. Where do we find him?

Perhaps writing becomes the stuff of legend because it wasn't invented but evolved. History, traditionally conceived of as the record of discrete events, of *happenings* and their causes, deals fitfully with evolutionary phenomena. Evolution isn't an event but a process, irreducible to names and places. It's distributed, occurring in many places simultaneously; and gradual, not likely to produce sudden perceptible transformations. And from this blind, implacable creation arises all the clamor and caprice of culture.

Writing's effects are radical: its emergence, its intimate role in consciousness, its very appearance, all strike at the roots of language, memory, and civilization. And that's what radical means, of course—it's from the Latin *radix*, for "root." Letters and signs can look like roots pulled from the ground in their tangled skeins of lines and loops—dredged up from the dark, they nourish and support the meaning we cultivate in words. In semantics, a word's uninflected meaning is termed its "radical." Chinese dictionaries are organized according to fundamental graphic units out of which characters are compounded; the Chinese word for this is *bùshǒu*, or "index character," but in Chinese-English dictionaries, these base characters are called radicals. The Chinese themselves have in the past compared written characters to the bones of the dead, which like roots go in the ground. In that image there is the sense of written signs as the vessels or domiciles of our ancestors, skeins and baskets in which their essence is caught, carried, and revealed.

Digging Up the Roots

What are the roots of writing? What makes it look the way it does? Despite vast differences in their appearance and in the systems that govern them, most forms of written characters share profoundly similar traits: they're made of lines that cross, connect, and loop, and they arrange themselves into linear sets. Why is this the case? Why don't we have writing systems that convey meaning by, say, color or hue, or size, or relative location? It's easy to forget that much of what writing looks like is determined by the limits (or the possibilities, which is how I prefer to think) of our physiology. But those limits are dynamic; they respond to change by changing themselves, and create new possibilities as well. From the geometric designs inscribed on Neolithic pots to latter-day corporate logos, signs share a flexible and familiar graphic grammar, a topology of line.

Underlying the riotous diversity of writing systems, the essential shapes or configurations—we could say the true graphic roots—of the conjoined marks that compose the letterforms are remarkably few. The cross, the circle, the line (to name most of them) together give scope to considerable meaning-laden variation.

It has been suggested that the source of these configurations consists in the junctures or overlappings of forms in the human visual experience. The skeins of roots and limbs in the forest; the long curl of the river across the plain; the scatter of tracks made by birds in wet sand; such perhaps are the templates (or better, the muses) of writing. But is topology significant? Are we somehow "tuned" to be especially discriminating about topological arrangements? Is there something unique about the human visual equipment that raises or compounds the significance of junctures of circles and lines, makes figure stand out from ground?

Speculation about the roots of perception glosses over the basic history of graphic signs: whether alphabetic or ideographic, they start out as pictures of things. The fundamentals of perception provide a basis for understanding why writing works for us, and why it has conserved these signs so well over these three millennia. It's remarkably conservative, the alphabet, at a root/radical/topological level. And this, too: characters don't evolve only to be seen and read but made. Written. And the line is a handy tool for this kind of making. Aren't we makers, we manipulative specimens of *Homo faber*, seeking after all to remake the world and one another?

The question might be phrased like this: Are letters like roots, or are they more like flowers? Are they, in other words, fundamental units of meaning, as they often enchant us into believing; or are they blossoms, at once beguiling and spectral, which individual imaginations issue forth in order to invite others to take up our stories and ideas and reproduce them?

Evolutionary psychologists, who focus on the persistence of atavistic and primitive cognitive traits, argue that the brain did not evolve for reading and writing, and thus its adaptations to that purpose are somehow incidental. By the same lights, the spinal column's role in supporting our vertically aligned trunk and head for bipedal terrestrial locomotion is incidental to its "original purpose." Perhaps we were never *meant* to read and write. But this is like saying that we're not "meant" to be bipedal because the spinal column didn't originally evolve to support a large cranium atop the body of a striding, erect land mammal; that our ancestors should have never left the seas—let alone stood upon their hind legs and started telling one another stories.

In 2008, neuroscientist Stanislas Dehaene and his colleagues at Paris' Hôpital Pitié-Salpêtrière discovered that reading takes two pathways through the brain: a quick ventral path for fluent reading of familiar passages and a slower, parallel dorsal path for decoding unusual or difficult-to-read words. The trade-off between the two isn't seamless but has thresholds, like triggers, which are set at different points for readers of different expertise. Presumably, it's reading itself—especially during developmentally critical periods—which sets these threshold triggers. And this is not a case of two roads diverging in a wood—the brain hasn't simply chosen the low road of neuronal efficiency over the longer high road with its crags and switchbacks. It uses the one to prepare the way for the other; and when a word requiring more scrutiny arrives at the mind's gate, it sends it over the high road so as to watch it, learn a bit more about its tics and routines.

It's the remarkable thing about the brain, this capacity to change, to ramify, to complicate itself. It presents us once again with the chicken-and-egg question, however: if it takes brains raised on reading to produce fluent writing, how do we get writing in the first place? The brains that created it, after all, like our mythological Thoth, were illiterate, reliant on the naïve dorsal pathway to visually decode symbols.

How did the living thread of reading and writing find the quicker route through the bottom of the brain? Why did it take so long for the impulse to write to thread itself through the brain in this way? What were humans doing with their brains during the long centuries before the advent of writing? For many of those centuries they were engaging in symbolic behaviors of richness and complexity: honoring their dead, creating stone blades of elegance and symmetry far beyond the call of mere utility. They were probably singing, almost certainly dancing. And they were drawing and painting, prolifically and sometimes prodigiously.

Among the most famous and astonishing examples of ancient graphic arts are the cave paintings of Europe. Beginning about 32,000 years ago, Paleolithic people across what is now Western Europe filled caverns like those at Altamira in Spain and Lascaux in France with images of game animals, predators, and sometimes, themselves. Lascaux cave alone contains some two thousand images. These prolific artists of the Paleolithic continued to draw in their dark, smoky caverns for more than 20,000 years—a record of continuous cultural production that may be unmatched anywhere on Earth save Australia.

The Europe of the Paleolithic artists was a dramatically different place from today's Continent, different even from the primeval land of forest and field that Romans found when they crossed the Rubicon, and in which the myths and tales of the northern peoples are set. Stone Age Europe was much colder; the Gulf Stream that gentles modern Europe's climate today was deflected to the

south, leaving the peninsula bathed in Arctic air. The fierce tem-
peratures banished trees to the south, creating vast grasslands from
Britain to Kamchatka—and even beyond, to Alaska and northern Canada. Called the "Mammoth Steppe" by paleoanthropolo-
gist R. Dale Guthrie, this vast ecosystem was populated by large,
fur-laden mammals—mastodons, bison, shaggy wild horses—and
the predators that hunted them—saber-toothed tiger, cave bear,
and man. Humans hugged the southern fringes of this enormous
biome, where valleys like that of the Dordogne sheltered glades
of oak and alder, where the rivers ran and hills gave some shelter
from the northern winds that howled down the endless treeless
expanses of the steppe.

Since the nineteenth century, anthropologists have sought
meaning in the works of the Paleolithic artists. Some have seen
the dreams and trance-induced visions of a shamanistic culture.
Others have struggled to perceive in Structuralist rhythms of
pairing and opposition a kind of beastly grammar modulating
the meaning of auroch and red deer, of dun horse and mammoth; they have argued that the many thousands of paintings at
Lascaux tell a single coherent myth (what that myth is, they can't
tell us; these are paintings, not writing). But Guthrie, whose *The
Nature of Paleolithic Art* challenges the assumption that cave
paintings primarily treat of the supernatural, argues that they
represent the fascinations and keenly developed observational
powers of adolescent males in a hunting culture. Guthrie lives
in Alaska, where he not only studies prehistory but hunts and
fishes for his family's subsistence; he knows that hunting furnishes more than enough numinous experience without recourse
to shamanistic trance.

In place of trance-induced mythomancy, Guthrie finds a wealth
of natural-history detail: artists represent seasonal changes in the

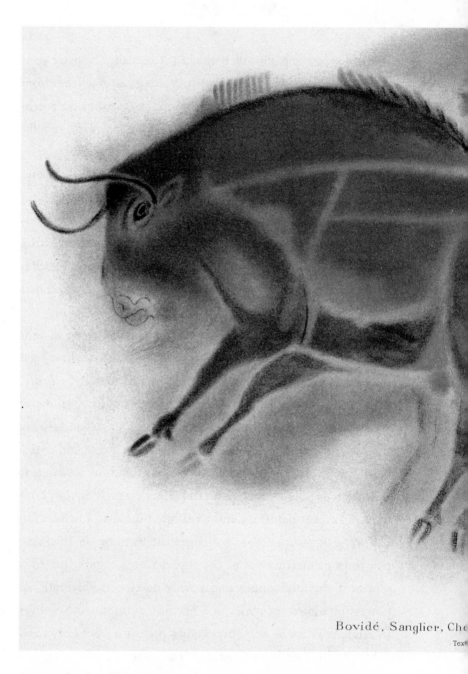

Bovidé, Sanglier, Che[...]

Tex[...]

Painting by the Abbé Henri Breuil, an archaeologist and Catholic priest whose depictions of the cave art from Lascaux and Altamira introduced the world to these remarkable works of art. This plate, which appeared in a book on Altamira authored by Abbé Breuil with Emile Cartailhac, takes the form of a hoofed palimpsest, with bison, boar, and horse forms superimposed. Cut

signes rouges

away from the petrific materiality of the cave, daubed onto the austerity of a white ground, and reprinted by offset lithography, Abbé Breuil's delicate and faithful images from Altamira evoke and transform the astonishing freshness and force of Paleolithic cave art.

coats of horses and deer; flicking tails and open mouths charac-
terize animals in rut or courtship. Such details would have been
significant to hunters striving to know such large and dangerous
prey. The cave painters' portraits of animals are most striking when
their detail and naturalism is compared to portraits of human
beings, which are fewer in number and much more rudimentary.
Where this disparity has been cited in the past as giving evidence
of a less evolved sense of human identity, it may be simpler to chalk
it up to the conditions of Stone Age life: in small societies, individual differences are not so notable, but a hunter's understanding of
the differences among his prey must be more keen.

But more important than observation, Guthrie argues, is the
role of sheer imaginative energy in cave art. Many images of ancient
game animals (and the much less frequent human figures) found
in the caves of the Dordogne are magnificent enigmas, apparently
fully realized; far more abundant, however, are the sketches, essays,
and incomplete doodles of casual ancient artists. Guthrie thinks
that much of what these artists were up to was the entirely familiar, perennial pursuit of play. More than a way to pass the time,
play is adaptive; through it we accustom ourselves to novelty and
calculation, learn to predict outcomes, and to intuit the motives
of others. For a large-brained species like our own, play offers a
degree of pleasure—which hardly contradicts, indeed entirely
results from, its profoundly practical nature. Yet in the joy it yields,
play becomes an end in itself. Our playful activities take place on a
razor's edge between the dictates of natural selection and the costly
wages of obsessive behavior.

Picture it: deep in a cool, damp cave during the warm season,
when flies buzz and the steppe turns marshy and soft. There is little for the young men to do—the herds have left for the northern

plains, and their fathers have followed them. By flickering tallow light, they snicker and jostle, dipping fingers into mounds of colored earth and dabbing them on the walls. *Here is the deer I will kill next year,* one says. *It is calling its mate. It doesn't know I lie watching it from the long grass.* His friend works quicker, catching up gobs of ochre and smearing them on the walls in a rough sketch: swollen breasts, round belly. *Here is my quarry,* he says. *I caught her while you were off wooing the stag.* They laugh and shove each other, their boasts rising as steam from the mouth of the cave.

It's been widely observed that in many ways, many characteristics of humans evolved by degrees of infantilization. Called *neoteny*, this lengthened juvenile phase allows us to behave childishly as long as possible, extending our cognitive and social powers into far-flung realms. Children love to elaborate upon rules; they concoct elaborate cants, codes, and mythologies of their own ephemeral devising. Like writing, play makes large demands. And yet humans do it everywhere all the time, spontaneously and irrepressibly. The bewilderment adults often feel at the strange ways of children is a by-product of neoteny. In an important sense, culture, language, the arts, and writing have their roots in extended childhood.

But the art of ancient Europe's cave painters did not give rise to the writing of today. Five millennia pass between the last painters in the Dordogne and the emergence of writing on the other side of the Mediterranean. The Danube Basin and other places in southeastern Europe have yielded evidence of a culture that made marks suggestive of calendars and other meanings—but they emerge thousands of years later, and are at best cousins many times removed from the Paleolithic artists of southwestern Europe. The connection I want to draw between the painters of the Paleolithic and the first scribes is not causal or even chronological; instead, we should look for ways in which all of these mark makers, widely separated by time and culture, answer similar problems and respond to similar urges. Before the practical conveyance of information or the skillful telling of tales, the mark makers come together in the more basic urge to play.

The search for the angelic script, the writing of God, the hermetic formulae, the primordial and originary inscription, has taken several forms. It has been sought in the vagaries of mysticism and prophetic insight; others have looked for it in alchemical ratiocination, the formulaic and algorithmic manipulation and recombination of existing symbols to reveal their ideal forms; and they have been sought in archaeology, in the traces of deep time found buried in the earth, or the practices of cultures with perceptible connections to ancient ways of life. The mapping of coastlines made by modern Inuit people of the circumpolar north, like ancient cave paintings, offers evocative suggestions of the human impulse toward graphic representation—and the desire to look for primordial traces and concoct just-so stories about the meanings of signs.

In 1884–85, Danish explorer Gustav Holm led an expedition to reconnoiter the east coast of Greenland. He pushed farther north along that coast, making contact with numerous previously unknown communities of Inuit. Among the qualities of the people that Holm noted, their geographic fluency struck him particularly forcibly. "The Ammassalik, like any other Eskimos, have a particularly sharp eye for nature," he wrote. "A place they have visited one time, even if it be twenty years back in time, they could describe very carefully, and they could provide a picture of it on paper, even if they have never drawn before." But one Inuit man in particular took things further: "The section (of coast) between Sermiligak and Kangerdlugsuatsiak a pagan named Kunak carved in wood,"

Holm reports. "Seen in the illustration is a reduced reproduction of these wooden maps on which the coast is continuous from one side of the block to the other, while outlying Islands are reproduced on the stick, on which the connecting pieces of course must be conceived omitted. The stick must gradually be moved as you explain the map, shifted to position islands in the right place." The accompanying illustration in Holm's book depicts a pair of charismatic objects: one planklike wooden artifact, its long edges deeply dentelated with fjordlike notches and insular knots; another, more sticklike, exhibits a series of toothy capsules along its length.

The above quote in translation is the extent of the documentation Holm gathered about these so-called wooden maps and their use; today, they reside in the Greenland National Museum and Archives in Nuuk. And yet they've developed a rich place in the history of the cartographic imagination. In a recent book on design and communication, they're taken as the primitive ideal for the expression of ideas in robust, transmissible, practical form:

> Imagine that you were kayaking along the coast of Greenland, and needed a chart to find your way. You might have a paper chart, but you will probably have trouble unfolding it with your mittens on. . . . You probably can't get cellular service where you are in your kayak. And even if you can, your battery is probably dead because it is so cold. . . .
>
> Now let's look at a third approach, one that the Inuit have used . . . two tactile maps of the coastline, carved out of wood. They can be carried inside your mittens, so your hands stay warm. They have infinite battery life, and can be read, even in the six months of the year that it is dark. And, if they are accidentally dropped into the water, they float.

All of this is true, up to a point. For in fact so little is known about the Ammassalik wooden maps; Holm's account doesn't even give measurements of the pieces, and no subsequent scholarly article I have seen offers a complete description of them either. More crucially, no other substantial examples of such maps made by the Inuit, near Ammassalik or elsewhere, appear to have been collected. From the scanty record, it would appear more likely that Holm's "pagan," pestered for something maplike, rather enterprisingly came up with an artifact that he thought would impress the bewhiskered European. And yet these evocative objects have managed to attract quite a bit of power to themselves as symbols of the symbolic life, as it were; one even appeared on a Greenland postage stamp.

We've searched long-sealed caves, ancient desert mounds, and fractured memorial stones for the roots of writing; everywhere, we find fully formed human imaginations already at work. Just-so stories about the Ammassalik maps betray some of our deepest assumptions about the origins of consciousness and its manifestations in symbols and things in the world. We keep looking for easy narratives lacing the primitive to the progressive—but the closer we look, the more we find that it's human complexity all the way down.

Tabula Rasa

The first writing system, known to the modern world as cuneiform, arose in Mesopotamia during the fourth millennium BCE, most likely in the city-state of Uruk. The ancient scribes didn't call it "cuneiform," of course; this Latinate term was first used to describe ancient writing by the Romantic literary scholar William Taylor in 1818 ("the cuneiform character is so simple in its component parts," Taylor wrote, "that it consists only of two elements, the wedge and the rectangle"—just as the Roman alphabet is simple, consisting merely of the dot and the line). The Sumerian word *sataru*, "to inscribe," named the act of writing as well as its effects, becoming in time a metaphor for the fame of kings.

Cuneiform would come to be ineluctably associated with the rise of civilization, with martial, economic, and governmental power ramified and elaborated upon as never before in the human career. Its beginnings, however, were more modest. Farmers and herders in the villages of the Fertile Crescent sought a means by which to count and track their herds and harvests. They did so by making use of materials abundant and close to hand: the rich mud of the Tigris and Euphrates Rivers and the reed—our bending, wayward, ever-youthful friend, known as Kalamos by the Greeks—which grew along the banks. For thousands of years they made tokens of clay to count their holdings. And *pace* Eric Gill, the earliest characters took shape as pictures *of* things; even in today's abstract and decadent alphabet, written figures resemble tracks and trees, bones, houses, and ants.

And then something happened. At some point in the last centuries of the fourth millennium, someone mixed counting and marking with picture making. Although its first uses were for accounting, it was not tallying alone that drove the emergence of cuneiform. The glamor of image making exerted its influence through the rough figures representing sheep or talents of grain, and a kind of marriage commenced between sign and concept, which spread to link and encompass figuration and the word. The marvelous cosmos of mark-making possibility—a world lost and regained every time a mind connected to a hand picks up a stick on the beach—link by link, glyph by glyph, merged with the copious universe of things and words.

From digging and scratching in dirt and mud, the numerate writers of Mesopotamia graduated to cutting their reeds in wedge-shaped cross-section and pressing the end into the soft clay to make neat, sharp-edged marks, and to combine them cleverly into signs for things, concepts, and ultimately words and the sounds and parts of speech.

How did it happen? It's impossible to know for certain, of course. But as mark making grew in economic importance, it would have been taught as a skill to children, the prototypes of the scribal academies we know from the literature of cuneiform itself. And here, perhaps, the neoteny we find among the Paleolithic artists comes into play. As children are exposed to such things, they transform them; through play and idleness, through scribbling and doodling, they enlarge and extend them. In a closed, hierarchical society like those of the burgeoning proto-cities of ancient Mesopotamia, the playful and absentminded children of one generation grew to become the scribes and the teachers of the next generation; some small part of their own scribbling play—the fittest figures, the most attractive signs and structures—could have been seamlessly inscribed as innovation. It may seem farfetched, this image of writing's emergence as a product of children's play. And yet in a vastly different time, using vastly different tools and media, a similar dynamic is flourishing today. It goes by the name of social media.

In the three millennia that followed its emergence and rapid development, cuneiform would undergo many changes. It would come to be inscribed not only in clay but also wax, stone, metal, and even paper (in the form of papyrus). The medium in which it was born was ancient—people had been scrawling images in mud for tens of thousands of years—and of course pottery by this time was an ancient craft in the Fertile Crescent and beyond. But the mud and clay that gave cuneiform its distinctive style would, in the wake of its obsolescence, become utterly foreign to the literate hand. Today, it's all but impossible to bring into focus the strange sensorium of the Mesopotamian scribes—with the smell of earth heavy in the air; the slip, or liquefied clay, drying and cracking on fingers and clothes; the rough adhesive texture of the damp linens used to swaddle unfinished texts between sessions of scribal labor.

The latter-day strangeness of the clay medium makes it hard to conceive of cuneiform not as a kind of media dead end or a primitive stepping-stone to the more advanced alphabet, but as the fully formed writing system it was: ancient in its lineages, supple and sophisticated, clever and complex, able to express multiple languages (even in some cases simultaneously). The Sumerian tongue is what linguists call an isolate; it lacks clear relationships with any known language family. Through the long centuries of turmoil and transformation, Sumer became the sacred and scholarly language of Mesopotamia, giving way to Akkadian, Elamite, Hittite, and others—Semitic and Indo-European languages that had little in common with the original Sumerian. The drive to shape cuneiform to new languages drove constant innovation and created a need for symbols that expressed not only words but sounds and modes and parts of speech.

The question is not why writing emerged, or how it managed to do so despite enormous odds against it. Instead it's this: what took it so long? For in a larger sense, writing is utterly natural to the plastic fantastic that is the human brain. We don't need writing to be

fully human, but full humanity means that the emergence of writing is always and everywhere possible, even likely. Our brains make minds by virtue of their ever-ramifying expression of cultural possibility. Once we see writing in this way, it's easier to be sanguine about the irruptions and transformations of written expression. It's in the nature of writing—it's in the nature of cultural things—to change, to break and remake themselves. Technological transformation in the modes and manner of reading and writing is not a rupture, but the expression of writing's inevitable, inexorable life as a cultural thing. It's not the specific changes but change itself that is the necessary thing. And writing has been changing all along.

So curiously, where I've been trying here to describe the situation at the dawn of writing, I end up concluding that we're always poised on writing's cusp, always tipping into invention.

FACING PAGE: *Ishtar on a lion, a god on a mountaintop, a supplicant whose piety is kissed by the crescent moon: a tiny scene unrolls from this example of a cylinder seal, a key variety of scribal tool in the Mesopotamian world. In a world of meticulous and messy writing media, the cylinder seal was a convenient tool for quickly bestowing a signature on a document. In two lines of Assyrian cuneifrom, "Belonging to Ubashi-..., eunuch of Piqitti-ilima," this seal accomplishes its quotidian task. Yet it accompanies this ostensive and prosaic pronouncement with a scene of tender complexity. Unrevealed to the reader, the most delicious secret: the smoky chalcedony of the seal itself, a stone that seems to glow with a feral inner light.*

PICTURES AND THINGS

Writing begins in China at about the same time it first appears in Mesopotamia. The exact starting point is veiled, contested. The origins of Chinese writing, like those of writing in general, are bound up in an essential paradox: the best evidence for writing is found in writing itself. Characters mass on pages, walls, and screens like ever-multiplying forests, the traces of their beginnings secreted in serifs and flourishes like rings within trees.

For the Western eye, the problem is compounded when turned to *hanzi*, the characters that comprise written Chinese. In form and usage as well as the sheer number of glyphs, Chinese writing is so utterly different from alphabetic writing—and yet so utterly recognizable as writing—that it has prompted a great deal of the fascination and puzzlement Westerners have often reserved for Asian culture. In its fascination, the occidental imagination inclines eastward—in ways that have both troubled and enriched cultures East and West. The uncanny mystery of writing has seemed, to certain

Westerners in certain times and places, more glamorously, prom-
isingly, and troublingly encoded in *hanzi* than in more familiar
writing systems. For these are characters speaking to and through
our eyes in ways that would seem to unsettle the streaming, lin-
eal, wavelike ebb and flow of language in the medium of the
alphabet. Language arrived through alphabetic writing in waves
of discourse, while *hanzi* seem to light up as individual novae
of meaning-making intensity. Alphabetic characters, it is often
assumed, are particulate and elemental, something less than fully
determined in their individuality, but in aggregate closer to the
living vectors of language, bobbing on the stream of discourse like
flotsam on the waves. *Hanzi*, meanwhile, seem like visual insular-
ities of expression, pictures of things, at once closer to meaning's
bone and more alien to the flickering, warm life world of language
itself. But to describe things this way is already to partake in occidental fantasies about Chinese writing that have long goaded and
bedeviled encounters between East and West. In the traces of the
living history of Chinese writing, we find much that is at once
more mundane and more wonderful than the orientalist fancies of
questing colonials.

The earliest Chinese writing, the "oracle bone script" of the late
Bronze Age's Shang dynasty (as early as the fourteenth century
BCE), also called "shell and bone" script, was used in divinatory
practices now called scapulimancy, pyromancy, and plastromancy.
These fortune-telling rituals required that questions be engraved
into the scapula of an ox or the ventral shell (or plastron) of a
tortoise, then laid in a fire or pressed with hot pokers, the bony
material cracked in patterns connecting and cleaving the written
message. While this earliest Chinese script is named today for the
divinatory arts with which it is associated, it was not devised for
fortune-telling but for the fluent expression of language. It emerges

not as a fragmentary picture-writing practice but a fully formed system for recording the whole of the language.

Writers of the Shang period also used brushes and ink, and incised writing into clay for later casting in bronze; it seems that the preponderance of oracle bones in the material history of early Chinese writing tells us more about the longevity of bone in the archaeological record than it does about the full range of uses to which early writing was put. Although inscribed on large, flat expanses of bone, oracle script is typically composed in vertical columns, which seems to indicate that writing on strips of bamboo, well documented from later periods in early Chinese history, was already a practice in the late Bronze Age. In all likelihood, Chinese writing matured in the centuries at the start of the second millennium BCE in media more ephemeral than the bones of the ox and the turtle.

Oracle-bone script appears in ancient China at roughly the same time as cuneiform does in Mesopotamia. The question of which system comes first, and whether there is some link between them, has long been contested. But one thing is clear: in both cases, writing emerges in full, committed not to ideas or images but to *language* in all its complexity and flexibility. The *hanzi* (Han characters) of modern written Chinese descend from this system, which from very early on consisted in thousands of glyphs representing not only pictograms but ideograms, phonetic characters, and compounds of these—in short, every one of the several ways of organizing modern Chinese characters already existed in the middle of the second millennium BCE. Chinese characters would undergo many transformations over time, continuing through the twentieth century—and yet in its sophistication, abstraction, and complexity, writing emerges around the Shang court of Anyang in Henan Province seemingly fully formed.

A percentage of *hanzi* are pictograms: pictures of things in the world. Such symbols aren't the traces of some more primitive, picture-based stage of symbolic activity but the product of a mind already conversant in abstraction. For a pictogram is a picture of a thing made conventional—in a sense, a picture that refuses to be a depiction. While a drawing of a horse in the caves of Altamira or Lascaux, by contrast, may exhibit certain conventional elements—a privileging of the profile, refined techniques for rendering mane and tail, a preference for running poses over standing or grazing—in each case, such conventions are manipulated with expressive individuation. Whether a drawing represents a single animal is almost beside the point; regardless of the artist's representational intentions, the drawing is ineluctably the trace of an individual event of artistic composition. A pictogram, by contrast, is a picture not of a single thing but a kind of thing. It arrives as an analysis, a mapping, and a classification. Of course, a drawing is also a thing, and a complicated one at that, transcending mere representation to participate directly in the world not merely mimetically but charged with sense, story, and a sense of occasion. But the nature of that participation is generally less fungible than is the case with the pictogram. It's worth remembering here the observation of the type designer Eric Gill, that making a letter isn't drawing a picture of the thing, but making the thing itself.

Ideograms are pictures too, but of ideas, not things (perhaps this, too, is an invidious distinction—for what is an idea but a thing, and how can we know what an idea is except through the things it makes and changes?). So the ideogram, like the pictogram, is conventionalized—but the things depicted are found in the mind. Such signs include some of those most favored by Westerners intent on explaining the nature of Chinese writing and its role as a medium of literary expression. A canonical example would be *Tŏu,* "to shelter," which suggests the lid of a pot. Here we have perhaps the reference to a thing,

although a thing idealized or modeled rather than recalled, used here metaphorically, grasping at the form that an idea takes in the mind. Deployed as a radical, or constituent element, in compound characters, such ideograms do often modify one another in poetic and telling ways—as in the character *Xiāng*, "to rejoice," which places the *tou* radical over the characters for "child" and "mouth."

Characters also manifest purely phonetic traits. Chinese is a language rife with homophones and near-homophones, and in many cases archaic characters survive as signs for sound-alike words without any graphic connection to the things or ideas at stake. And the pictorial, semantic, and phonetic get combined in artful ways as well, in compound characters—such as the character for *chōng*, or "flush," which combines the radical for "water" with the character *zhōng* ("middle," as in *Zhongguó*, the central country or Middle Kingdom, one of the traditional names for the Chinese nation), which is present simply as a clue to the pronunciation of the word. While this sounds complicated, the majority of *hanzi* are formed this way—and are read and written by literate Chinese with no more need to parse the etymology and iconography than an alphabet user needs to dot an *i*.

FACING PAGE: According to the catalog entry in the Harvard Art Museums, the inscription reads as follows: "In the King's tenth month in the third quarter on the day jichou, *the King proceeded to the Temple of Geng Ying and awarded ten strings of cowries and one box [?] of cinnabar. Geng Ying in order to extol the King's graciousness had made for her accomplished mother-in-law this precious vessel. May sons and grandsons for ten thousand years and forever after treasure and use it." Ten thousand years. It appears inside the lid of a bronze wine vessel cast during the Zhou dynasty, nearly three thousand years ago already, close to the beginning of the first millennium BCE. I get lost in its topography of patination, its archipelagos of crazed bronze and blooming verdigris, which deliver fresh and in full the weighty millennia that are denied by the writing itself, with its combination of matter-of-fact reporting and dynastic ambition.*

What's striking about the completeness and complexity of the earliest Chinese writing is how directly it flies in the face of Western presumptions that have arisen about the nature and origin of Chinese writing in particular—presumptions also at work in our intuitive sense of the development of writing generally and, even more broadly, about the emergence of abstract systems out of concrete and pictorial representations. It's easy to tell just-so stories about the emergence of written signs from pictorial representations of things in the world; but—as we've seen with our earlier rebus-writing experiments, the recursiveness, abstraction, and sheer complexity of conveying meaning through written means quickly multiply the challenges to developing a written system out of pictures. But the challenges of written Chinese, which both produce and constrain its special effects and creative potentials, are rooted not merely or even primarily in the play of its complex graphic systems but in its social distribution and use. And for a Chinese author writing in English, it is the social dimensions of *hanzi* that have peculiar force.

Retreat Immediately

The title story of Ha Jin's 1998 collection *The Ocean of Words* concerns Zhou, a recruit in the People's Liberation Army in the early 1970s. Zhou has a secret: he reads, and even keeps, books—a dangerous habit in the midst of the Cultural Revolution. When a rival rats him out, the political officer, Director Liang, secretly lets Zhou continue his studies in his private residence. Zhou pesters him to understand why he breaks the rules to help him, and Director Liang responds with a story. During the war with Chiang Kai-shek's Nationalist Army, Liang had led a machine-gun company. He was ordered to hold a hilltop while the main body of the army retreated, and await orders. The next day they fought a great battle but held the hill. That night, a messenger delivered orders: a scrap of paper with two characters on it. "I turned the paper up and down, left and right," Liang tells Zhou, "but couldn't figure out the meaning. I shouted to the whole company, 'Who can read?' Nobody answered. In fact only the party secretary could read, and we had lost him." After conferring with his officers, Liang decides to hold the position. The Nationalists attacked again and again, and many of his men were killed before the company was driven off the hill. Liang lost his arm in the fighting. And when he and his few remaining men straggled into the retreating army's camp, Liang's commander nearly killed him on the spot: for the two characters in the order had said "retreat immediately." "You see, little Zhou," Liang concludes, "just two small words, each of them cost sixty lives. Sixty lives! It's a bloody lesson, a bloody lesson."

Ha Jin's story furnishes a telling example of the manifold importance of writing. In the first instance, the didactic nature of Liang's anecdote frames writing at its most functional, in this case serving the violent establishment of a totalitarian regime. A political, state-making move like this is bound up in the origin stories of writing, with Mao here in the position of the Mesopotamian kings of old. This rough-hewn tale of the costs of illiteracy is a tale figured *in* writing, justifying writing's ways to its audience both through its purported moral and through the pleasure and impact of its presence as a thing made of written words. And—crucially in this case—that impact serves to call the state-making power of war and totalitarian control into question.

Ha Jin, a justly celebrated expatriate novelist, himself served in the Chinese Army. The tales in *Ocean of Words*, which concern the bleak affairs of PLA soldiers stationed on the tense border between feuding China and Russia in the second half of the twentieth century, have been described by critics as revisiting the territory of Isaac Babel's *Red Cavalry* stories. But Ha Jin's own story—and his relationship with language, literature, and writing—are starkly different from those of the doomed Russian author. Babel, martyred in the madness of the Stalin regime, is remembered as a master of Russian literature, one devoted to the rhythms and tensions of his native language (although it might be wiser to reserve that term for Yiddish in Babel's case; he also composed stories in French, a gesture much favored by Russia's pre-revolutionary literati). Ha Jin, by contrast, who came of age in the Cultural Revolution, made a radical commitment to become an author not in his native Chinese but in English (and at a time in his life when he was far from fluent). In this connection, Ha is perhaps more immediately comparable not to Babel but to Vladimir Nabokov, whose lapidary English is the product of a similar choice and refusal rooted in both literary and political impulses.

Aesthetically and politically, Ha Jin's refusal of Chinese as literary language is a deep and doubly freighted move. For in it, he not only sets aside the immense literary patrimony of China's classical tradition but also offers a rebuke to the incredible strides made in literacy during the Communist era in China. Under Mao, a mass-literacy program emerged to rival the world-defining exploits of the emperors of old. In a series of moves throughout the 1950s and '60s, the government of the People's Republic introduced simplified versions of thousands of Chinese characters. Attempts had been made at simplification before Mao came to power; in the 1930s, the Kuomintang government of Chiang Kai-shek had introduced some three hundred simplified characters in an early attempt at systematically spreading literacy.

But it was the Communist revolution of Mao Zedong that

brought literacy—and with it, simplification—to the masses, with a control over the administration of society unmatched since the days of the first emperor, Qin Shi Huangdi. More than any other force in Chinese history, the revolution was conveyed and prosecuted through writing. In palm-sized pamphlets of cheap paper and banners the size of buildings, the Communists put their message of liberation into writing. Despite its ties to the elite civil-service system of imperial China, Communist authorities sought to harness the power of calligraphy rather than consign it to the dustbin of history as an aristocratic vestige. Mao was a dedicated poet, composing verses even during the dark days of the Long March; his calligraphy was held in special reverence (the masthead of the *People's Daily* is rendered in a version of his hand). Yet in the interest of expanding literacy, he even considered turning to Romanization—the transcription of Chinese words into alphabetic characters, which is used frequently in Western contexts by students of the Chinese language—to extend the reach of written language to peasants and others long denied access to literacy by the imperial system.

Mao's simplification effort, which began in 1952, aimed to reduce both the total number of characters and the complexity of many individual glyphs. The number of strokes was reduced; homophonic words were made to share characters; component characters were omitted entirely; and in some cases, simpler archaic forms were reintroduced. This last technique illustrates something crucial to understand about the simplification process: while remaining legible and recognizable to the learned, Chinese characters have been changing their forms and styles throughout history, from the earliest bronzes of the Shang dynasty to the oracle-bone script to the proliferation of seal scripts and calligraphic styles of classical Chinese.

In Taiwan, where calligraphy is supported with government money, the Nationalists made a point of eschewing simplification, signifying thereby a connection with the scholarly traditions of Chinese culture. Yet Taiwan enjoys universal literacy using traditional characters, undermining the claims of simplification. In a number of moves in recent years, the Chinese Communist government has reintroduced traditional versions of many characters.

The complicated turns taken by writing in the history of modern China, however, are remote from the interests of most Western observers, who long have preferred to impute to *hanzi* qualities they associate with the East: mystery, abstraction, and decadence; but also immediacy, wisdom, and power. The fancies inspired in occidental thinkers and artists have not only fueled misunderstandings between East and West but have inspired epochal transformations in Western art and literature.

The *Chinese Recorder* (1871), a newsletter for Western businessmen associated with the China trade, offered an explanation of the character *chuan* for the word "ship." Radicals comprising the character include *pa*, meaning eight; *ko*, meaning mouth; and *chou*, for boat. To a soberly protestant, business-minded writer of the mid-nineteenth century, such a figure evokes the image of Noah and his family—thus the character seems to support the authenticity of the Christian story of the Flood: "Why should this idea be found in the character for ship," writes the *Recorder*, "unless at the time of the formation of the character there had been a tradition about the Ark in which Noah and his family escaped?"

But Chinese thought and writing reached deeper into North American Victorianism than the fancies of investors in clipper ships. Ralph Waldo Emerson, for one, famously was influenced by his reading of Eastern ideals, especially those drawn from Confucianism. A chief resource for the Confucius-curious, English-speaking reader in the first half of the nineteenth century would have been the *Elements of Chinese Grammar* by Joshua Marshman, which contained a translation from Confucius known to Emerson, who transcribed from Marshman's version of the *Sentences* in his journal.

In the early nineteenth century, when few Westerners yet understood Chinese, Marshman shows that a mythical sense of the pictorial foundation of *hanzi* —the "Imitative system," as he calls it—was fully in place:

> To some it may be interesting if we enquire *what* objects among those of sense have been selected, for the sake of forming the basis of this medium of communication: and though we can scarcely imagine, that, while most of the languages formed on the Alphabetic plan bear evident marks of being formed rather by accident than design, a number of Chinese sages should have sat "in deep divan" in order to select certain objects as the basis of the Imitative system, we shall yet find these elements include most of those objects of sense which are remarkably obvious; few being omitted, which from their form or frequent use might be likely to attract notice. They include the most remarkable objects of nature, as the sun, the moon, a river, a mountain, fire, water, earth, wood, stone, &c; the chief parts of the human body, as the head, the heart, the hand, the foot, the eye, the ear, &c.; the principal parts of a house, as the roof, the door, &c. as well as those utensils most frequently in use, a knife, a spoon, (or chop-stick,) a seat, a box, a staff, &c. . . . Such are the Two Hundred and Fourteen Elements, which are justly esteemed the foundation of the Chinese language.

Marshman's cataloging of the 214 "elements," called radicals today, is accurate enough; this subset of characters, which are used in combination to form thousands of other *hanzi*, has been the settled basis of Chinese dictionaries since the seventeenth century. Marshman's account would turn it into a kind of mystical system as well. On the question of origins, Marshman fixes on mythical beginnings:

> The Chinese in general ascribe the invention of the characters to *Fo-khee,* to whom they also attribute the institution of marriage, the introduction of clothing, &c. Some however, give the honor of the invention to *Ts'hang-kih*; while others say that he merely improved the characters invented by *Fo-khee.* Still, respecting *Ts'hang-kih* they are divided in opinion; some esteem him one of *Fo-khee's* ministers, while others place him in the reign of *Hwangtee* the inventor of the cycle (of sixty years) and of certain useful arts. *Ts'hang-kih* is said to have resided in *Yang woo,* and to be buried in *Lee-hyang.* ". . . *Ts'hang-kih* was a man of extraordinary capacity: he was acquainted with the art of writing even from his birth. . . . One day with a tortoise, and observing its shell distinctly and beautifully spotted, he took it home, and thence formed the idea of representing things around him. Looking upward, he carefully observed the figures presented by the stars and the heavenly bodies: he then attentively considered the beautifully variegated shell of the tortoise, the wings of birds, the form of mountains, rivers, &c. and at length formed the written characters." It is added, in the genuine oriental stile, that when the characters were formed, heaven poured down food in abundance, and the evil spirits filled the night with howlings.

Concluding his account, Marshman adds a note of perplexed ambivalence about fitting the notion of mimetic drawing to the variety, abstraction, and idiosyncrasy of *hanzi* in toto:

> The reader will judge for himself relative to the degree of credit due to this ancient tradition; but the first efforts of this kind were probably attempts to delineate the *objects of sense* around. Whether such imitations would bear any likeness to the thing represented, is another question: that this would be intended, seems more than probable; but that the resemblance should be in many cases so exact as of itself to demonstrate the object represented, is scarcely to be expected. Nor is anything of this kind intended to be affirmed respecting the elements. They are laid before the reader simply as *Elements*; and every man will judge for himself respecting any real or imaginary resemblance between the *head*, the *hand*, the *heart*, the *mouth*, and the characters by which these are represented.

In their estimations of Chinese, Western thinkers manage at once to celebrate its terseness and compactness and to identify the shady, ambiguous, vague, and obfuscating style of the "Oriental." The character of Chinese poetry especially strained the Western sensibility to breaking—and much of the puzzlement lay in the confrontation with *hanzi*. Again and again, nineteenth-century commentators fixed on the writing. John Francis Davis, in his *Poeseos Sinicae commentarii*, a substantial early English-language discussion of Chinese poetry, recounted that when his treatise first appeared, in the 1830s, written Chinese "was so little known in England, that Lord Palmerston, with his usual pleasantry, said he took it 'at first sight for a work on *Entomology*'. . . . A notion seems to have existed, that the whole merit of Chinese poetry lay in some curious and fanciful selection of the characters, with a reference to their component parts. As a medium for the communication of ideas, the written language certainly differs from the alphabetic systems: but, after all, the characters are the *means* only, and not the *end*. The melody of the sound—the harmony of the structure—and the justness of the sentiment, or beauty of the imagery—constitute, as they do everywhere else, the merits of poetical composition." And yet these sensibilities are often expressed with a compactness striking to Western minds. In his journals, Emerson compared Chinese poetry approvingly to that of children's speech, noting that "we use ten words to one of the child's," while "his [the Chinese writer's] strong speech is made up of nouns and verbs, and names the facts." And while Emerson does not make the leap here, the connection between the primordial and the simple, the Adamic and the childlike, is a strong one; and Chinese writing has often been read by Westerners as a system that combines these qualities.

Emerson's debt to South Asian thought is well known; he wore his contact with Chinese thought more lightly. Not so his protégé Thoreau, whose work is soaked not only in the virtuous discipline of Confucius but also the holistic vibrancy of the Tao. "Instead of engineering for all America," Emerson said of Thoreau at his funeral, "he was the captain of a huckleberry party"—with engineering as the ordering and regulation of Confucian ethics and berrying as the woodland-wandering way of a Taoist holy man. Emerson wished his protégé had attended more to the discipline of Confucius and spent less time dilating in hazy wonder. In fact, however, Thoreau's enthusiasm for Asian culture was rooted in his reading of Confucius. He recorded a translation, from Paultier's (French) edition of *Confucius et Mencius*, of a favored anecdote in which Confucius asks four of his followers what they would do if they were to become famous. The first two describe great achievements in governance; the third wishes to lead through clerical achievement and ritual. The fourth, Tian, strums a few notes on his guitar, then describes going off to bathe in the river with friends and enjoy the fresh air. "For the most part," Thoreau writes in the unpublished version, "when we listen to the conversation of the Reformers, we are of Tian's mind." Some have questioned Thoreau's Confucianism, but it stems from the particular engagement he had with the classics, in the form of the Neo-Confucian Four Books, produced in the Sung dynasty, rather than the older canon. The Sung scholars who compiled these later, revisionary works, living in a time of political turmoil, stressed the Confucian ideal of self-improvement as a means for social and political betterment: to cultivate first the self, and then others. As scholar Hongbo Tan points out, Thoreau's huckleberry picking and self-cultivation can be seen as the outward marks of a world-bettering agenda that he found confirmed in Confucian philosophy.

For Emerson, Thoreau, and many of their contemporaries, these effects of Chinese thought were remote and abstract, far removed both from living Chinese and the vital complexity of their written language. In the twentieth century, however, Western writers became more immediately familiar with China's culture and peoples. The peculiar and momentous way in which occidental moderns experienced freshening and estranging effects in Chinese writing is perhaps nowhere more efficiently expressed than in Ezra Pound's poem "In a Station of the Metro":

The apparition of these faces in the crowd;
Petals on a wet, black bough.

In this famously swift-spun distich, Pound sought to overturn the ornate lyricism and patterned, hieratic, lapidary prosody handed down to the twentieth century from Victorian verse. Pound's austere, deft apposition prefigures the uncanny edict with which William Carlos Williams set the tone for poetic high modernism: "no ideas but in things." (If written characters are things, they are the objective means by which poetry dreams its way into the material realm.) For such poets, explosive and imagistic immediacy would become a chief virtue in the early twentieth century, and the influence of that revolution is still felt today across the fragmentary, hyperlocal worlds of poetry in the twenty-first century.

The transmission of Pound's metonymy here—two metonymies, really, set alongside each other, each one earning its peculiar force from the other—at least in part evokes the construction of certain *hanzi* as well, in which radicals with pictorial roots combine like mathematical factors in a dense, ramifying formula. It's no surprise, then, that in the same year this poem was published (1913, in *Poetry*), Pound received from the writer Mary McNeill Scott a manuscript bundle of notes by her late husband, Ernest Fenollosa, on the workings of Chinese written characters. Struck by the ramifications of Fenollosa's theory of *hanzi* for making poetry and for limning its nature and impact, Pound reworked the late scholar's notes into a book called *The Chinese Written Character as a Medium for Poetry*. Its influence on modernist poetics— and upon Western notions about *hanzi* and Asia—would prove deep and long-lasting.

Born in Salem, Massachusetts, Ernest Francisco Fenollosa was the son of a Spanish musician named Manuel Fenollosa and Mary Silsbee, the daughter of one of Salem's oldest seafaring families. Ernest graduated first in his class at Harvard in 1874, his years

there coinciding with an efflorescence of interest in art at the
college; Charles Eliot Norton would become America's first professor of the history of art in 1875. Boston as a whole was alive
with interest in the arts at that time, with the new Museum of
Fine Arts opening its school, and wealthy Bostonians such as Isa-
bella Stewart Gardner traveling the world and returning to the city
with works from Renaissance Europe, the ancient Mediterranean
world, and the Far East.

Through a Salem connection, the newly married Fenollosa was
offered a teaching appointment at Tokyo Imperial University in
1878. This was the height of the Meiji Restoration, which had
begun with fall of the shogunate and the consolidation of political power under the emperor in 1868, leading to Japan's defini-
tive opening to Western contact and influence. The process was
active on both sides, with reform-minded Japanese not only looking to the West for new ideas, institutions, and opportunities but
seeking to fuse traditional mores with novel influences to create a
specifically Japanese take on modernity. As a teacher, curator, and
maker of art, Fenollosa cultivated precisely this fertile, ambiguous
territory between East and West. On behalf of the modernizing
imperial government, Fenollosa worked to document and preserve
temples, landscapes, and art across Japan, which were threatened
not only by rapid modernization but by the resurgence of old
nationalist prejudices against Buddhism that led to the seizure and
desecration of temples and holy sites. Smitten with the aesthetics
of old Japan, Fenollosa strove to preserve and update the arts and
crafts. Adopted into the ancient Kano lineage of artists, he helped
to define the *nihonga*, or traditional, style of painting—a genre
meant to be complementary to newly Westernized pictorial styles.
And yet in his teaching, he sought to reform art training by replac-

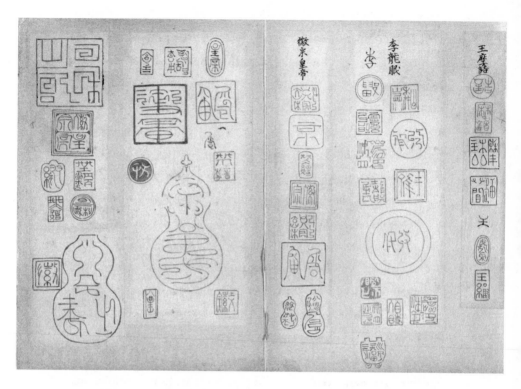

Fenollosa was a vigorous collector and compiler of the written arts of East Asia, especially in China and Japan. Among his archives is this album of seals expressing the signatures of Japanese artists and Chinese literati, which conveys traces of authorship that interest philologists and a palimpsest of forms of written expression. Expanded and transformed by Pound, Fenollosa's ideas about the written Chinese character transformed Western poetics. Fenollosa's own approach to the written, however, had its careful and curatorial dimensions as well, expressing a healthy, patient attention to the forms as they present themselves—not as universal poetic emissions but as irreducibly individual acts of expression.

ing rote copying with the vitality of working with live models and *en plein air* composition.

Fenollosa returned to the United States in 1890 to teach, lecture, and head the new Department of Oriental Art at the Museum of Fine Arts in Boston. In the next two decades he became an impresario of encounter between the arts and cultures of East Asia and the Occident. Although inclined to mysticism, Fenollosa was no naïve exoticist smitten with the mystery of the Orient; to his thinking, East and West were embarking on a grand, historically determined process of cultural fusion, which would eventuate not only in open markets and cultural tolerance but a new metaphysics as well. And in the early years of that century, his mind bent toward *hanzi* as a writing system capable not only of typifying this syncretic mentality but of bringing it into being.

For Fenollosa, the word was not the thing, but a means to it; his ultimate interest and object wasn't poetry per se but human engagement and understanding in full. His own experience of Asian culture was born in a time of Western expansion and renewed cultural conflict between East and West; Fenollosa's hope for a rectification of names wasn't literary but political and spiritual. The encounter of Occident and Orient should be "no conquest, but a fusion," he wrote in an article for *Harper's* in 1898 called "The Coming Fusion of East and West":

> We are not to court Japan for the number of her battleships, nor China by the tonnage of her imports; rather to challenge the East soul to soul, as if in the sudden meeting of two brothers parted since childhood. It is primarily a test of ourselves, whether we are capable of expanding local Western sympathy and culture to the area of humanity.

Fenollosa thought of Chinese writing as a nearly perfect system of signs that could not only resolve the ambiguities, the absurdities, the essentially arbitrary nature of language, but also order thought itself better than language seems to do—in a fashion closer to reality, closer to the ideal forms. As scholar Haun Saussy puts it in an essay on Fenollosa's linguistic metaphysics, "A language so organized by 'natural suggestion' but not 'abstract' would make possible a permanent *zheng ming* [. . .] or 'rectification of names' (a term from Pound's translation of the *Analects*), with, as Fenollosa put it, 'no possible confusion of the real meaning.'"

When Pound took hold of this idea, he gave it the twist of his peculiar, paranoid economics: to him, language strayed into a kind of usury when it roamed beyond the concrete into modifiers, tenses, and logical operators. Through Fenollosa, Pound began to see in Chinese written characters a system in which such flights of spendthrift fancy were impossible.

The power of the Chinese character as a medium for poetry was typified for Fenollosa, and for Pound, by the existence of compound ideographs, which combine two characters to produce another, and often seem to work through simile, synecdoche, or even compact narrative. Perhaps Pound's favorite example was the compound ideograph for the word *xin* 信, or "trust" or "truthfulness," comprising *ren* 人 for person (in its radical form, 亻) and *yan* 言 for speech. There is the sense in this compound of a person standing by his word—a formulation not attributable to Pound or even Fenollosa, but to Xu Shen, the second-century lexicographer whose etymologies continue to be influential. For Pound in particular, the image of a man standing by his word could be taken to represent the action of the Chinese written character itself: written words willing to stand beside things in the world, not covering over that which they signify or merely pointing to things, but standing by them.

After Ezra Pound brought Fenollosa to the attention of his coterie of followers and rivals, the notion would become a dominant strain in American poetics for the rest of the twentieth century. And while serving as the basis of a revolution in poetics, Pound and Fenollosa's interpretation of the Chinese character also underscored understandings of Chinese writing as an esoteric and atavistic system at the service of a conservative, decadent elite.

The notion of a "rectification of names" means something different for Pound than it did to Confucius, however. In the *Analects*, Confucius describes the rectification of names as the maintenance of proper relationships, the ongoing discipline of creating and maintaining community. For Pound, by contrast, the rectification of names promises at once to purify decadent, routinized forms of poetic address and to restore writing to its originary intimacy and immediacy of address. This brings Emerson to mind again, and his notion that "all language is fossil poetry"—in which words emerge with lyric, even heroic force, which in time is undone by instrumentality—an instrumentality made possible by writing and its replacement of the primacy of oral speech.

In editing together *The Chinese Written Character* from manuscripts given to him by Fenollosa's widow a decade after their composition, Pound further distorted the nature of Chinese writing. Fenollosa was a man of the 1890s, and his tastes showed the mark of Impressionism. He wanted a syncretic, synthetic theory to unite East and West in a blur of color. His metaphors for artistic effect, his examples from Western poetry, tend toward détente between East and West. But Pound wanted nothing of concord or agreement; he was out to tear down the canons of tastes in Western poetics. He didn't need to make Western art more like Eastern; he wanted to remake all art at once. And so he removed from Fenollosa's work the material that didn't suit the hard, constructed clarity of his Imagist movement, along with Fenollosa's consideration of sound in poetry and his open attitude toward Buddhism. Pound saw the Buddhist influence in Asian art as soft and decadent; Saussy suggests that this attitude hearkens back to Matteo Ricci, the seventeenth-century Jesuit missionary who saw it as strategically useful for Christians to give support to Confucian morality and to criticize Buddhism. Buddhism enlivened Fenollosa's understanding of the arts, however; he was electrified by the image of Indra's Net from the Flower Sutra: a crystalline structure comprising the web of all causal relations, which is also "the sentence that would take all time to pronounce." Pound couldn't use it: he needed the thing itself, divorced from its interpenetrations with/of/by all other things. Sometimes a wet, black bough is just a wet, black bough.

A superficial irony: in his attempt to shake loose the death grip of Western poetic tradition, Pound turned to an even older tradition (as he would again and again, making particular use of medieval troubadour poetry in his churning search of the new). And yet Fenollosa and Pound leave out so much of the complexity, cultural richness, and expressive force of classical Chinese poetry, with its lineages of literati; its elaboration of strict syllabic metrical modes and thematic genres; its music, rooted in the semantic rhythms possible in a largely monosyllabic, tonal language; the logical and narratological structures unique to the tradition; as well as the historical ebb, flow, and interpenetration of voices, styles, techniques, and occasions for composition. For all its misbegottenness, however, the book Pound made of Fenollosa's hopeful notes helped fuel a revolution in poetry throughout the twentieth century. As

Haun Saussy points out, "the ambiguity as to what makes Chinese a model for poetic language has been unpredictably fruitful": the Objectivists, Beats, and Black Mountain poets, the work of William Carlos Williams and Allen Ginsberg, Louis Zukofsky and Gary Snyder, Robert Creeley and Robert Duncan—all trace inspiration from the compounding, productive misprision of Fenollosa and Pound.

In an important sense, Fenollosa and Pound's enthusiasm for the powers of the Chinese character initiated a new appreciation for Asian culture, one more firmly founded in respect than earlier, suspicion- or superiority-fueled waves of Western *chinoiserie*. In a West caught between fears of a "yellow peril" on the one hand and a smug estimation of Asian decadence and passivity on the other, Fenollosa's conviction of the necessity of Asian culture in the historical unfolding of consciousness in the world ensured that *The Chinese Written Character as a Medium of Poetry* would place not only *hanzi* but the entire matrix of civilization from which they spring on a more even basis with the writing traditions of the West.

Through Ezra Pound, Fenollosa furnishes modern Western poetics with its modern conception of Chinese: unpacking the imagistic content of characters furnishes access to etymology, to the "authentic meaning" behind words. It hearkens back to dreams of a universal language of sign and symbol freed from the baggage of culture and tradition, offering a direct connection between the mundane world of things and the ethereal realm of ideal form. The troubles with this view are manifold: it robs from us the chance to come to grips with the metrical flex and architecture of much Chinese poetry; it essentializes Asian culture in a way that impedes, and doesn't promote, mutual understanding between Asian and Western people. And finally, it misunderstands the nature of poetry's entanglement with writing and language. Ideographic decipherment offers all the pleasures of puzzle solving, but none of those of poetry.

Chinese culture, of course, developed its own tangled just-so stories about the origins of writing. "One method anciently and effectively used by the Chinese themselves," scholar John Hay writes, "is the imagery of the organism, of physiology as we would classify it. Brush strokes have 'bones' and 'arteries,' characters have 'skeleton' and 'sinews.'"

Hay states that authorities on calligraphy traditionally have described script with such qualities as *jou, chin, ku, hsueh, mo, feng, chi,* and *shen* (flesh, sinew, bone, blood, vein, wind, breath, and spirit). As Hay points out, the import of such terms is never self-evident, but yields complex meanings embedded in the very fabric of the Chinese sciences of health. In classical Chinese understanding, there was no dichotomy such as anatomy/physiology. The body was not a set of meat parts set into motion but a zone of overlapping spheres, the "interplay of systems." The word "liver," for instance, refers not to the material organ as such but to the "sphere" of energy and functions for which the liver serves as structural basis. And the boundaries of health extend beyond the corporeal; "In figure painting," Hay writes, "it was clothes rather than flesh which proved the most suitable medium for representing patterns of energy." All is transformation; even solid bone is a manifestation of *chi.* Change, resonance, rhythm, pattern—such basic categories of Chinese perception were prone to rich elaboration in aesthetic theory and the practice of the arts.

In Chinese medicine, the workings of the body are transformations taking place in a microcosm, a world within the world, reflective of the whole, a vast system with flows from above to below, trickling down from the wider domains through realms of the infinite to the particulate. The movement of the brush is calligraphy-in-the-making, an action thing that distributes or disperses energy, "a Yang function," which is akin to Heaven; the *structure* of the character, meanwhile, the very form it takes, is no mere image but a thing, substantial, like the Earth itself. Ever in the making, the word is composed of concrete, in-the-world elements (brush, ink, paper). Writing shapes these substances into invocations by means of the movement of the brush, a transmission from the realm of the ideal.

The ancient Chinese arts of health and the modernist poetics of Pound and Williams share a fascination with possibilities expressed in connections among words, written characters, and things in the world. This fascination finds expression in science as well: in 2006, a team of brain scientists argued that diverse writing systems exhibit "empirical regularities in the shapes of letters and other human visual signs," which give us evidence of "underlying principles governing the shapes of human visual signs." The authors examine three classes of sign systems—alphabets, *hanzi*, and nonlinguistic symbols such as icons and logos, find broadly distributed similarities in what they call "sign topology": the schematic arrangement and relationship of the strokes and volumes of written characters. Such similarities, they argue, emerge thanks to evolution; shapes develop in response to a selective pressure that favors their susceptibility to visual perception and discrimination over the ease of their mechanical production.

They're talking about topology: the abstract, underlying geometrical arrangement of strokes, distinguished from variations in the thickness of lines or relative size of loops, whorls, and serifs. Topologically, a *P* and a *q* are equivalent, as are a coffee mug and a doughnut. (This isn't strictly true in the typeface in which this book is set, however, as the bout of the *P* doesn't close to make a counter.) The range of topological variation is much smaller than that of graphic or even geometrical variation. "Any environment with opaque, macroscopic objects strewn about," they point out, "will possess strong correlations" with the topology of signs found in visual systems. The researchers marshal impressive data and geometrical arguments to make their case—and yet it seems to add up to another just-so story, one tuned to the vogue for evolutionary explanations of human behavior. Patterning and consistency would seem de rigueur in writing systems—without these qualities, they wouldn't be systems. If writing evolves readily from such basic facets of the human visual experience, we have to ask why it didn't emerge ten or one hundred thousand years ago, instead of so recently in the human career. The imputation of fundamental topological unity across sign systems seems instead like an act of pareidolia, that trick of hyperconscious human visual thinking that brings us the man in the moon and the face of Jesus in the tortilla. And yet our capacity for pareidolia, too, likely contributes to the flourishing life of writing in the human career.

We're back to the "books in running brooks" and "sermons in stones" in the pastoral vision of Shakespeare's Duke Senior. But for the topologists, this pastoral vision isn't limited to the planet Earth, but is shared with extraterrestrial life as well. "Informally, we expect that if there is intelligent alien life, then so long as they live among macroscopic opaque objects strewn about, they will probably have a configuration distribution that is somewhat similar (to ours)."

Why is topology significant? Methodologically, the investigators feel it's a safe bet because "any given human visual sign can undergo significant variability in its geometrical structure without losing its identity, but typically, its topology cannot vary." Thus we have sans serif, bold, cursive, block, gothic, half-uncial, oblique, italic; in *hanzi*, "grass-style," seal script, bronzeware script, as well as printed forms in sans-serif and block styles—a nearly infinite spectrum of variation, across which topologies, the "deep shapes," as it were, remain constant, and constantly legible.

And the creative possibilities of those characters extend beyond pictography and topology into even more eccentric geometries. The fact that Chinese may be read in any direction has been exploited by poets in a traditional genre called *hui-wen shih* or "reversible poems"—anagrams taken to a new level of multivalent complexity. The acknowledged masterwork of the genre, the fourth-century "Star Gauge" or "Armillary Sphere" by Su Hui, consists of a grid of more than eight hundred characters arrayed in regions and meridians, evoking the mechanical models of the heavens from which the poem takes its name. At its center, the character *hsin* for Polaris— also for words "heart" and "mind"—was left out of many editions, as the nature of the heart in Taoist cosmology is emptiness. What's extraordinary about "Star Gauge" is the sheer combinatoric prolixity of its many readings: the characters can be read in nearly any order; as long as the generic rule of dividing it into quatrains of seven-character lines is observed, some three thousand poems are permutably possible. Some of these embedded, enjambed poems strike notes of lost love and wounded passion, while others are statements of cosmic exploration.

Su Hui was a woman, and there is a kind of just-so story about her composition of the poem: her husband, a magistrate posted to a far-flung locale, took a concubine, and Su Hui made the poem to win him back. David Hinton, the translator and anthologist of Chinese poetry, thinks this is a fable dreamed up by male scholars. "It is clear," he writes, "that the poem is much more than a woman's plea for her husband's return. It is a complex philosophical statement, as well as an assertion of her own dignity and even superiority to the men who dominated her world. 'Star Gauge' reads like a vast collage, lines juxtaposed almost randomly, a compositional strategy that would not reappear until . . . 500 years later, and not in the West until the 20th century."

This collage of combinations, this written expression of passion and precision, seems at once coolly abstract and intimately human. I want to say we're wired for writing—although it's more evocative (and possibly even more accurate) to say that writing employs our wiring to express itself in the world. Were we wired to see like dragonflies, our writing would take altogether different form. And yet writing is of *our* world, not that of dragonflies. There are no natural scenes, no standard configurations, without our particular perceptions. Our world is woven from the weft our fibers weave. And in this world, letters are not windows or conduits or frames for some more vital reality; they are things in themselves. Like armillary spheres and other well-wrought artifacts, they're both made by and making human culture; where one picks up and the other begins can be impossible to tell.

For all its topological salience and geometric complexity, writing is linked to language. Writing-like modalities that are not rooted in language (ideographs proper, icons, logos) are on the other side of a divide from writing. They are free in ways that written things are not. Writing does partake of these freedoms, the freedom of the graphic—it's what gives us typography and calligraphy, all the expressive possibilities exploited by designers, sign painters, and scribes. Yet their free acts all play out against the ground of language, the word, which stands on the other side of writing from us. A visual "pun," a hidden sign, as well as a sense of rhythm, of contrast, of vigor or languor in lines—these being aesthetic phenomena—all play with and against language as a figure to ground. Or perhaps they appear behind language, evanescent and uncanny, a luminous screen against which play the shadows of the word.

Topology rather instrumentally describes the foundations of signs, the way arithmetic can account for conglomeration and dissolution. Left out is the capturing action of consciousness, the presence-to-mind of form playing across both apparent and subliminal landscapes of cognition, which culture and experience take up and iterate upon endlessly.

Writing is a perceiving-through: a look through a window, or more properly a lens (for of course even a window is already lens, however subtle its refractions). One forms letters while attending to something that stands beyond them. In this sense, the written character seems to act everywhere as allegory—alphabetical or ideographic, Western or Asian. We're back with *xin* 信, with "truth" as the tale of a little man who stands beside his word. Or maybe a little man imprisoned by it—for in *yan* 言 not only is the image of a mouth but perhaps a house, even a cage—like the one that held Ezra Pound at the end of World War II when he was imprisoned by the U.S. Army for treason at a detention center near Pisa (a cage into which he was allowed to take three books besides the Bible, on the understanding that they were his religious works: a text of Confucius, its English translation, and a Chinese dictionary). The trouble with the rectification of names is that one person's picture, one person's truth, is never wholly that of another; each of us stands beside our own word in witness or advocacy.

Xu Shen's etymology for the compound character, upon which so much of Pound and Fenollosa's hopes were hung, has been called into doubt. In the case of *xin* 信 ("trust"), the *ren* radical is now interpreted as a phonetic marker—a kind of pronunciation hint—and *yan* as the signific. Recent scholarship deprecates the whole notion of the compound character in favor of a theory of character construction much more supple, shifting, and provisional, based on imagery to be sure, but also homonymy, mnemonic juxtaposi-tion, and the accretion of arbitrary associations.

Like the rectification of names, the fusion of East and West, which Fenollosa predicted more than a century ago, turns out to be fraught, provisional, and perpetually in the making. In the place of the rectification of names, I prefer to think instead of Fenollosa's favored image of the Net of Indra: in each character, a reflection of the entirety of the universe. . . . I'm reminded of a short story by Jorge Luis Borges, about a man who can't bear to have his house torn down because it contains an "aleph"—a singular place from which all other points in the universe are visible. The Aleph א, of course, is the first letter of the Hebrew alphabet, the character for a glottal stop or hiatus—that pause in the stream of speech in which, for a fraction of a second, any meaning is possible.

WRITING AND POWER

What think you I take my pen in hand to record?
The battle-ship, perfect-model'd, majestic, that I saw
    pass the offing to-day under full sail?
The splendors of the past day? or the splendor of the
    night that envelops me?
Or the vaunted glory and growth of the great city
    spread around me? —no;
But merely of two simple men I saw to-day on the pier
    in the midst of the crowd, parting the parting of
    dear friends,
The one to remain hung on the other's neck and
    passionately kiss'd him,
While the one to depart tightly prest the one to remain
    in his arms.

—WALT WHITMAN, "CALAMUS"

Writing Lessons

Deep in the Amazonian jungle of Brazil's Mato Grosso state, Claude Lévi-Strauss was in trouble. Traveling with a small band of Nambikwara, the anthropologist knew the group was riven with internal discord. They had not wanted to accompany him into dangerous territory; Lévi-Strauss had to purchase their chief's complaisance with beads and other goods. But as the group set off in a classic explorer-in-the-jungle train of mules and straining, box-toting porters, the chief's people remained wary. A couple of days later, the chief lost the trail; searching a new route, the party nearly ran out of food. While they rested, the chief and his wife had gone into the jungle, collecting baskets of grasshoppers, which they brought back to feed their restive band. Despite this, nerves remained on edge. And now fearful, stuffed with grasshoppers, and cold in unfamiliar territory, the group had blundered into a meeting with a rival band. Warriors stood in the gloom fingering their weapons, eyes alight.

With the threat of violence hanging in the night air, Lévi-Strauss persuaded his chief to begin an exchange of gifts. Among the anthropologist's offerings were pencils and paper for everyone. Soon people had set their weapons aside and were busy "writing"—producing wavy lines, one atop another, filling the sheets of paper. The Nambikwara, Lévi-Strauss observed, were curiously mimicking the movements he made whenever he opened his notebook. But the chief, he noted, took the show a step further. Seating himself next to the anthropologist with his writing pad perched on a naked knee, the chief began answering Lévi-Strauss's inquiries, not verbally but by "writing" on his pad and then passing it to the astonished explorer. "He was half taken in by his own make-believe," Lévi-Strauss wrote; "each time he completed a line, he examined it anxiously as if expecting the meaning to leap from the page, and the same look of disappointment came over his face. But he never admitted this, and there was a tacit understanding between us that his unintelligible scribbling had a meaning which I pretended to decipher; his verbal commentary followed almost at once, relieving me of the need to ask for explanations."

As the exchange of gifts continued, the chief used his "writing" to buttress his authority as the middleman, consulting his pad as items were removed from one set of baskets and placed in others. "No doubt [the chief] was the only one who had grasped the purpose of writing," Lévi-Strauss concludes. He used it not to acquire knowledge or to increase understanding, but as a symbol of control, "increasing [his] authority . . . at the expense of others."

For Lévi-Strauss, this scene discloses crucial truths about the nature and function of writing. Rather than its avowed purpose of allowing us to record the past, learn from our mistakes, and share knowledge in the service of progress, writing everywhere has "favored the *exploitation* of human beings rather than their enlightenment." Lévi-Strauss points out that perhaps the most creative epoch in the human career, the Neolithic revolution—the period that saw the efflorescence of art and the domestication of plants and animals, among many advances—proceeded without the benefit of writing. Lévi-Strauss concludes that

> the only phenomenon with which writing has been concomitant is the creation of cities and empires, that is the integration of large numbers of individuals into a political system, and their grading into castes or classes. . . . My hypothesis, if correct, would oblige us to recognize the fact that the primary function of written communication is to facilitate slav-

ery. The use of writing for disinterested purposes, and as a source of intellectual and aesthetic pleasure, is a secondary result, and more often than not it may even be turned into a means of strengthening, justifying, or concealing the other.

In laying the ills of civilization at the feet of written discourse, Lévi-Strauss was following the example of his intellectual great-grandfather, Jean-Jacques Rousseau, for whom writing inscribes and makes official a defeat in a battle already long lost by the time writing makes the scene. The first language humans spoke, he reckoned, was the spoil of a primordial battle for meaning and freedom. In an elaboration on the myth of Babel, Rousseau figures that the very consonants and vowels went to war against one another, dividing and corrupting the universal language that all men spoke before the confusion of the tongues. "Natural sounds" in Rousseau's reckoning were "inarticulate"—howls and ululations, born of the open mouth. In the originary language of Rousseau's mythology, consonants interpose themselves across this natural soundstream, disciplining and ordering the voice so as to make it articulate. Out of such segmented ululation, words are born. The originary language "would have been sung rather than spoken," Rousseau conjectures; "it would deemphasize grammatical analogy for euphony, number, harmony, and beauty of sounds."

Before long, however, the consonantal complication of language runs amok. "To the degree that needs multiply," Rousseau writes, "that affairs become complicated, that light is shed, language changes its character. It becomes more regular and less passionate. It substitutes ideas for feelings. It no longer speaks to the heart but to reason. Language becomes more exact and clearer, but more prolix, duller, and colder." Writing for Rousseau emerges from this dynamic, progressive, metastasizing alienation: "Writing, which would seem to crystallize language, is precisely what alters it. It changes not the words but the spirit, substituting exactitude for expressiveness." With writing's advent, language ends its prelapsarian phase, trading oral language's mythopoeic effusion, innocent and promiscuous, for precision and fixity. This chilling exactitude is also a feedback loop: "The means used to overcome this weakness tend to make written language rather elaborately prolix; and many books written in discourse will enervate the language." Elsewhere, Rousseau explores writing's enervating, decadent influence on social life: "So long as government and the law provide for the security and well-being of men in their common life," he writes, "the arts, literature, and the sciences, less despotic though perhaps more powerful, fling garlands of flowers over the chains which weigh them down. . . . Necessity raised up thrones; the arts and sciences have made them strong."

Rousseau here is being more specific than Lévi-Strauss would be two hundred years later. The arts and sciences gild the chains of civilization; over our senses and intuitions about our fellow humans' needs and intentions they have imposed system, etiquette, *politesse*. Of the primordial past, he writes, "human nature was not at bottom better then than now; but men found their security in the ease with which they could see through one another. . . ." The arts and sciences—not mere observation and expression but the institutional practices of the liberal arts, foundationed upon writing—provide endless tools for restraining man's natural passions and occluding his perceptions. "Let those who will extol the moderation of our modern sages," Rousseau writes; "I see nothing in it but a refinement of intemperance as unworthy of my commendation as their deceitful simplicity." This is the mode for which

Lévi-Strauss's chief comes to desire writing: as a tool to bureaucratize his charismatic effects, and a mystifying glamor with which to bedazzle his fellows.

The Magisterium of Writing

Of course, it's not wonderstruck barbarians but spellbound readers who believe most fervently in the magical powers of the written word. Thinkers touched by writing tend to attribute to it a unique capacity to give voice to the absent and the dead—as if to precipitate progress itself from the base metals of stasis and complacency in which mankind toiled until writing paved a way out of primitivity.

But we seem to want to have it both ways. The richness and immediacy of orally based culture contrasts starkly with the ignorance and inaction in which the illiterate seem mired; the literate know memory, the law, and literature, but for it they lose the Garden of Eden. These two takes on writing rhyme with two major Western ways of understanding the past and human nature itself. Of which disposition is writing the handmaiden: Liberty, or Slavery? Progress, or Decadence? The triumph over a life nasty, brutish, and short; or the demise of the noble savage? The poles are irreconcilable; each breaks down in contact with the other. For hundreds of years, thinkers lined up on opposite sides of this ideological split.

But perhaps there is another way to understand writing's relationship to power and politics—a perspective that unites literacy to a broader conception of "reading" and "writing," not as specific behaviors but as fundamental human ways of making sense of the world and exerting power over it. For *power*, not communication or verbal art, is what concerns Lévi-Strauss in the "Writing Lesson" chapter of *Tristes tropiques*. Although it's a recent arrival on the human scene, writing is forever getting mixed up with the frontiers of the primordial.

To unsettle the idea of writing as revolutionary, we must first let go of the notion that human life before writing was either a static Eden or an endless war of all against all. Is history a uniquely written institution? Or was history happening long before writing's emergence? Power—the subject and product of our political behavior—enlivens mythical accounts of the irruption of writing, with written characters taking the form of mighty trees, armed warriors marching to battle, or the dead in judgment; letters springing from the earth, flying from the singing mouth of the creator, falling from the tree at the center of the world. Preliterate human struggles left their imprint in myth, in social and political forms, and in the body of writing itself.

For poet and novelist Robert Graves, the roots of writing's ancient power reach back to the myth-time of the Welsh, in whose bewildering, bloody tale-cycle, the *Mabinogion*, he scried a fable of writing systems at war with one another, with the letters as trees animated by a kind of literary magic to do battle with the forces of chaos. For all such effects and resonances, letters are nothing less than spells sprung from the deep places in our imagination. Far from liberating mankind from a mythical static stone age or enchaining us with its records and restrictions, writing is a means and a matter of enchantment. Of course, where there is enchantment, there are both songs and chains.

For all its utility for the wielders of power, writing also proposes itself as a kind of independent government of the human mind—a vast constellary system glimmering in the dark, providing guidance, charting the heavens, and inspiring new and ever-proliferating structures of imagination. *Government* doesn't seem quite right, though; writing is less a machinery of power and authority than it is a discipline, a mode, a school of thought. Beyond the rote-instilled rules of orthography and writing style, beyond the rule of punctuation, beyond the fruitful restrictions it imposes on thoughts in the form of word and sentence, chapter and verse, writing *teaches*. Its magisterium bestows lessons of patterning, of rhythm and remembering, out of which it yields meanings that don't so much direct as transform us.

We can't lay our expulsion from the Garden of Eden solely at writing's feet. Our means of self-domestication were too varied and subtle for that—and what is essentially wild about the human species may be expressed as well in writing as in hunting or sleeping or migration. There is no noble savagery for which to atavistically pine, any more than there is some ignoble savagery from which we escaped. Or this: there is always already ample savagery, noble and ignoble, and we'll never write our way out of it. Lévi-Strauss is right to point out that the Neolithic revolution was an intensely creative episode that took place without writing, beyond the reach of documentation by writing's means. And long before that, we can be sure, humans were striving, hating, imagining, and creating. Humankind filled up the African continent and then moved on to every other habitable landscape, compelled by familiar urges. This is our deep history, the history before historical documents— but the evidence is there to read this story in the bones, in the layers of the earth. *Written* there, as it were.

Feet of Clay

The traces of writing's origins are not only found in the earth, they're made of it. Cuneiform, which arose in the burgeoning city of Uruk in Mesopotamia, consisted of marks incised in clay tablets. Cuneiform would seem to confirm the jaundiced expectations of Rousseau and Lévi-Strauss: its earliest texts celebrate and tabulate the spoils of war—cities razed, enemies beheaded, concubines taken captive. From the first, scribes wrote at the king's behest; they were often slaves themselves. And yet almost from the very start, a subversive spirit animates the early texts. In mankind's first known literature, exemplified by the epic of Gilgamesh, doubt and moral vision intrude upon the triumphant hagiography of the kings.

The *Epic of Gilgamesh* tells the story of—well, of Saddam Hussein's precursor, the mythical scion of the line of self-made despots who ruled ancient Mesopotamia. The historical Gilgamesh probably lorded over the city of Uruk in the early part of the third millennium BCE, 1,200 to 1,500 years before the Trojan War. It's worth putting this in the perspective of deep history: Gilgamesh's story is set 5,000 years ago, more or less at the time of the invention of writing. This is the remote dawn of civilization to be sure; the Iron Age wouldn't begin for another 1,500 years. And yet human language was already perhaps 40,000 or 50,000 years old; anatomically modern *Homo sapiens* had roamed the planet for more than 100,000 years. Human beings already lived on every continent save Antarctica. In terms of the life of our species and the history of human culture, we and Gilgamesh are contemporaries. It's no wonder we continue to find resonance and relevance in his tale.

What's astonishing about *Gilgamesh* as a piece of writing is that this foundational text in world literature was lost, its abundant, allusive traces in other sacred and secular texts unnoticed, for 3,000 years. One Mesopotamian legend tells that Gilgamesh's grandfather Enmerkar invented writing (which he uses, much like Lévi-Strauss's chief, to cow rivals, issuing ultimatums and overleaping distances with his words). Gilgamesh himself reigned a few short generations before scribes began to expand the magisterium of writing by composing not only decrees and fortunes but literary texts. And the tales of this charismatic leader, perhaps the subject of then still-living memory, would echo throughout the Mediterranean lands, leaving their traces in Homer's epics and the Bible.

Five thousand years later, the discovery of clay tablets containing these stories written in cuneiform, which seem to outline the Old Testament, turned the Western world on its ear, as scholar of world literature David Damrosch recounts in *The Buried Book*. Like an archaeologist, Damrosch begins with recent layers, those closest to the surface. George Smith, a brilliant, self-taught Assyriologist in the mid-nineteenth century, was studying shards of clay collected near Mosul in latter-day Iraq by several British Museum expeditions, translating their syllables into English. The son of London laborers, Smith was an engraver who taught himself to read Assyrian cuneiform during lunch hours in the British Museum. One passage Smith happened to decode spoke of a "flood storm, a ship caught on a mountain, and a bird sent in search of dry land." Smith had found the earliest known analogue of the biblical story of the Flood, written down in Akkadian nearly eight hundred years before the birth of Jesus.

Smith rose to prominence with the discovery of *Gilgamesh*—the tale of the eponymous Mesopotamian god/hero and the earliest known work of literature, of which this version of the Deluge serves as the final chapter—and in one stroke made the archaeology of Mesopotamia a topic of intense public interest. His discovery came at a time of great unease in Christendom: the age of Darwin, when geology and natural history combined with an increasing knowledge of human diversity to present the West with a world different from the one explained by biblical tales—much older and more accidental. In the mid-nineteenth century, the race was on to show that the Bible's wonders and miracles were as real as Darwin's finches, as venerable as the bones of the Neanderthal. With Smith's discovery of a precursor to Noah, Assyriology went overnight from scholarly backwater to Victorian media sensation.

One of Gilgamesh's earliest and biggest fans, however, was Ashurbanipal, who ruled the Assyrians in the eighth century BCE. Unlike his father and most of the Mesopotamian kings who preceded him, Ashurbanipal was a fluent reader and accomplished scholar. Ashurbanipal created the first true library within the precincts of his palace, selecting and preserving not only accounts of his own glorious victories but something like a comprehensive collection of cuneiform texts literary, magical, and practical, conserved and organized with great care.

The Assyrian Empire fell to its enemies not long after Ashurbanipal's time; the palace was destroyed by invaders and the library of fired clay tablets buried in its rubble, their contents safely buried and forgotten. As David Damrosch observes, there is an irony here: in one act of destruction, *Gilgamesh* was both lost and preserved. Had Assyrian culture suffered a long decay instead of an abrupt and violent demise, the tablets containing the epic might have been subject to centuries of creeping neglect, during which time they likely would have been battered to dust.

In the time of its flourishing, however, with Assyrian power at its height and the magisterium of writing growing to encompass the eastern Mediterranean, Gilgamesh's story spread among travelers and traders. His wrath, his love for his boon companion, Enkidu, and his bottomless store of cunning have their echoes in the *Iliad*, while the cataclysmic flood lodged itself in the tales of the Israelites. Such story lines presumably flow through unseen channels from the deepest layers of human memory. One wonders how many forgotten stories' fragments lie flung beyond writing's reach, lodged within our heads, casting shadows on the tales we learn and tell. What other early poems lie hidden in plain sight, spliced into the very DNA, as it were, of Greek epic, the *Mahabharata*, the Mayan *Popol Vuh*, the Bible, and even fairy tales?

Ultimately, *Gilgamesh*'s biblical ties would prove to be of more literary than historical significance. For the epic would be read as the drama of a newly urban and self-domesticated humankind coming to terms with its loss of wildness. The hero begins as a headstrong, hubris-laden young ruler, building city walls and scattering enemies. But the pride of this son of the goddess Ishtar is too much—he demands droit du seigneur of his suffering subjects, sleeping with each new bride on her wedding night. To correct his ways, Ishtar sends him Enkidu, a wild man who, after initial wariness and struggle, becomes Gilgamesh's sidekick. The two share adventures as Gilgamesh subdues demons, digs wells, and seeks the secret of eternal life.

Gilgamesh tells us much of what we know about the mind of ancient Mesopotamia. But it is strong and supple literature as well, a story that served its original readers not only by providing instruction in kingship and burial customs but by speaking truth to power and exploring the ephemeral beauty of human life. In its vigor and sensitivity, this prodigal tale seems to set the pattern for so much of the literary art that followed; even Shakespeare's Prince Hal is prefigured in *Gilgamesh*, with Enkidu a young and sensitive version of Falstaff reminding his friend what may be gained by the building of walls and the razing of forests, and what may be lost as well.

Like his predecessors, Saddam Hussein was fascinated with *Gilgamesh* not only for the epic's promise of greatness rooted in ancient Mesopotamia but for the lessons it offers to those who would rule. Hussein authored (with the help of a ghostwriter) his own saga in novel form—another tyrant seeking to put writing's fickle powers to his service. His literary ambition is both instructive and amusing; but his was not the only regime to seek to rule the lands between the Tigris and Euphrates, nor was it the last.

Grapholexia

Since the time of Gilgamesh, the most powerful and widespread languages have been written ones, spreading and putting down roots in the consciousness of both conquerors and the conquered. In such cases, the magisterium of writing seems little different from the application of power pure and simple. The linguist Max Weinreich popularized an aphoristic explanation of the difference between a language and a dialect: a language, he said, is a dialect with an army and a navy. The power of such languages can persist long after the decay of the empires that birthed them.

Clearly, writing and power are deeply intertwined. It's as evident that not all written languages are equal; the capacities conferred or imposed by writing are not distributed equally in either expression or intensity from one forest of words to the next. Even (indeed especially) within the most extensively developed and massively ramified of written languages, such as English, there exist microclimates of expression, idiom, and custom—running from literary genres and vernaculars of commerce, office, and academy down to the flickering expressions of individual style. Such languages have their stratigraphy also; the dialects and rhetorics of earlier times lie buried in the archives, out of which seismic intrusions and upheavals—the discovery of *Gilgamesh* is one such eruption—occur with varying frequency and local intensity.

And then there are the scholarly and classical languages. Latin,

Greek, Sanskrit, and Classical Chinese, often derided as "dead languages," are hardly morbid in the same way as a language like !Xam, a Bushman language of South Africa whose last few speakers died in the first decades of the twentieth century. Perhaps the superannuated scholarly tongues would more properly be termed "zombie languages," where writing acts as the magic elixir that sustains their existence. But even among these, the variation is extreme. Classical Chinese, for instance, is the idiom of both poetry and the foundational texts of Chinese philosophy; it manifests a continuity of some three or four thousand years' duration. And yet within that continuity, as within the broad sweep of ancient Latin and Greek, there is marvelous diversity of genre, form, and style.

Historically in China, the connection between writing and imperial administration ran deep. Not only did the Chinese dynasties produce the longest record of continual governmental administration, the practice of calligraphy was also one of the four scholarly arts that comprised the training system of civil administrators. For a thousand years and more, one could not be a magistrate or other official without passing a grueling series of exams; continued felicity was required in calligraphy as well as poetry, instrumental music, and the game of Go—skills that still indicate the sensibility of the Chinese elite, the mandarin quintessence.

In the West, written Chinese has been understood as a language that divides its speakers into classes; the gulf between a tiny literate elite and the illiterate masses, it's often said, has been created and enforced by the difficult tuition of written Chinese. And yet with its compound of dense allusiveness, compacted vocabulary, and spacious syntax, the rudiments of Classical Chinese texts can be decoded by most speakers of the modern tongue with a felicity unthinkable for non-learned speakers of Western languages faced with Latin.

The poet and artist Henri Michaux had as sensitive an understanding as any Westerner of the beauty and power of written Chinese—a power not derived from emperors or parties, a beauty aloof to political and military might:

> These characters, illegible to hundreds of millions of Chinese, never entirely lost their meaning. Excluded from the inner circle of the literate, the peasantry looked upon these characters without, admittedly, understanding them, but sensing nonetheless that they came from the same place as themselves: those nimble signs, predecessors to the incurvated rooftops, to dragons and theatrical figures, to cloud drawings and landscapes with flowering branches and bamboo leaves.

Michaux points out that for those outside writing's magisterium, the characters may be formally meaningless and yet still alive—alive not only with the power of mystery, but with graphic force, with rhythm, with evoked symmetries in human forms, our life world, and all of nature. Alive with *meaning*.

In the end, nothing in the system of Chinese writing per se enforces imperial administration or ensures the place of an elite. Since the Communist Party came to power in the middle of the twentieth century, literacy in China has grown remarkably. And few forces in Chinese life have raised hopes and expectations more effectively than the expanding magisterium of writing—a power that leaders in all times and places have discovered makes a fickle servant, a faulty vehicle for their ambitions. The literacy that began in the People's Republic in the form of simplified characters on banners and in Communist Party pamphlets has grown into an Internet, fickle and unruly, which even under government authority continually eludes control.

Free Writing

In ancient Greece, however, writing arose among the relatively independent commercial class, traders and artisans doing business in the markets with foreigners and visitors from other cities. The alphabet emerged not in scribal colleges or the king's halls, nor was it brought by conquerors, but instead came ashore in the freewheeling, acquisitive, materialistic atmosphere of the agora, the Greek marketplace that also birthed democracy and the public sphere.

The Phoenician letters, transformed by Greeks into the alphabet, share an origin with the Hebrew characters; they crossed the Aegean Sea with trade that flourished between the Greek peninsula and the Canaanite mainland in the ninth century BCE. Phoenician traders frequented the Greek islands, while Hellenic trading colonies were established throughout the lands of Canaan—today Lebanon, Syria, and Israel; then the homeland of the Semitic Phoenicians. The first alphabetic inscriptions in Greek appear on goods—keepsake vases, containers for oil and olives. The likely earliest such inscription extant, the "Dipylon inscription," is on a wine jug; it reads something like this: "Whichever dancer dances most fleetly, he shall get me [this vessel]"—a trophy cup. The so-called Cup of Nestor, a clay vessel dating from the eighth century BCE, bears an inscription that begins "Nestor's cup am I, good to drink from." For the next couple of centuries, Greek letters are used mostly to inscribe dedications—indexing acquisition and ownership in a society where property was the basis of participation in the lettered public sphere.

This was a society of freeborn traders and artisans, a culture that prized beauty, expressiveness, and originality—the perfect environment for the kind of flourishing public space writing seems everywhere to wish to build. And yet the magisterium of writing grows slowly in ancient Greece. Centuries pass before the first texts appear. The dating of these poets is very controversial; Homer and Hesiod slip into myth, sharing priority with Orpheus as the earliest Greek authors. Hesiod mentions rivers first explored and prizes won by Greeks in the eighth century BCE, the era of the Dipylon inscription and the beginnings of the alphabet. Like Homer, Hesiod is replete with the formulas that facilitate memorization of oral epics: lists and epithets, rhythmic, repetitive phrases.

Signally, Hesiod begins *Works and Days* with a prayer to the Muses, "who give glory through song": "Through him mortal men are famed or un-famed, sung or unsung alike, as great Zeus wills." Here, the memory function writing serves is most powerfully evoked and connected to Zeus, the fountainhead of political might. Through song, the Muses bestow fame upon men—true to their origin as daughters of Zeus and Mnemosyne, the goddess of memory, patroness of the singers and remembrancers.

Homer, too, writes like an oral poet painfully aware of the limits of memory. As the classicist E. R. Dodds points out, when Homer appeals for divine aid in rendering his compositions, he asks for help not with form but content. "Always he asks the muses what he is to say, never how he is to say it," Dodds argues; "and the matter he asks for is always factual. Several times he requests information about important battles; once, in his most elaborate invocation, he begs to be inspired with an Army List—'for you are goddesses, watching all things, knowing all things; but we have only hearsay and knowledge.' These wistful words have the ring of sincerity; the man who first used them knew the fallibility of tradition and was troubled by it; he wanted first-hand evidence."

In what would later be called the home of Western literature, writing gets off to a supremely leisurely start. The classicist Eric

Havelock argued that Greek literacy requires a "special theory"; for there, as almost nowhere else, literacy arrives unforced. The artistic culture of ancient Greece had little need of writing; its power was held by the performers, the singers, to whom scribes and "authors" could appear only as rivals. Writing had even existed in Greece before the arrival of the Phoenician version of the proto-Canaanite alphabet—in the Mycenaean age from which the tales of Homer sprang. The Mycenaean writing systems, Linear A and B, derived from the cuneiform that already was ancient in the Mediterranean world. And they were used in the royal fashion of old, to serve ultimatums and record the deeds of the strong (or so it seems; Linear A has yet to be decoded). But between the Mycenaean age and the classical period, Greece underwent its own dark ages, and the letters were lost. By Homer's time, the oral poets who sang the tales of the Trojan War saw Mycenaean writing through a glass darkly; like the Nambikwara, they discerned the power of the marks but knew not how they were made to speak. Homer's only mention of writing comes in Book VI of the *Iliad*, which recounts how King Proteus sent his rival, the stalwart but unlettered Bellerophon, on an errand to a vassal king, carrying with him a "folded tablet" engraved with "baleful signs" and "deadly tokens" spelling out the doughty Bellerophon's own death sentence. This sole instance of writing in the *Iliad* dramatizes writing's old ways as a murderous servant of kings; moreover, it betrays an ignorance of writing's basic workings—for the tablet carries not words, but "signs and tokens." Rousseau was one of the first to point to this as troubling evidence that Homer was himself illiterate.

Havelock observes the irony of Greek literature: that the alphabet, which would replace the oral recitation of the bards, took as its first task the preservation of their oral culture. In Greece, the magisterium of writing took the form of a paradoxical "written orality" privileging acoustic aesthetics and public performance over the administrative needs of the kings. For all its vaunted powers of remembrance, writing seems to come into its own as art when it co-opts not only the bards' ancient task of recollection but the work of performance as well.

In time, Greek authors and scribes would compile whole libraries of texts, recording and performing in thousands upon thousands of scrolls piled up in Athens, Pergamum, and Alexandria. Those scrolls would burn and disappear, just as the tablets of the Assyrians had disappeared beneath the hills that overlook the Tigris and Euphrates. The Romans would follow their practice of library building. But writing, for all its powers of memory, crumbles again and again at the implacable forces of time, war, and change. Like Shelley's Ozymandias, the magisterium of writing always wants to say, "Look on my works, ye Mighty, and despair!" But it does so in letters that are forever crumbling into dust.

A Bestiary of Letters

Letters crumbled, were carved anew, and crumbled again for a long millennium before Charlemagne's great teacher, Alcuin, founded the school at Aachen, the favored royal residence in what is now westernmost Germany. From Aachen flowed a resurgence of classical learning that spread throughout Europe. Alcuin was born not on the Continent but in northern England, in what was at the time the Anglo-Saxon kingdom of Northumbria ruled by Æthelred I, whom Alcuin would later blame for a decadence and pettiness that left northern Britain prey to the long sundering season of the Vikings that began with the sacking of Lindisfarne, seat of the Bede the Venerable and an early home of monastic learning.

Writing and learning had holed up in Britain through the Dark Ages. In the sixth and seventh centuries, monastic scribal practices flourished in Ireland; monks made their way from the strife-torn Continent to learn Greek and imbibe the distinctive writing styles, or "hands," and the remarkable, intricate illumination traditions of the Irish scribes. Their brothers had traveled to England to found the monastery at Lindisfarne in 635, where their Hibernian scribal hands met and mixed with the half-uncial writing, descended from Roman cursive, that had arrived in Kent with Augustine in 597.

Secreted like jewels amidst the depredations of feudal warlords, the monasteries were isolates of order organized around writing— the slow, steady proliferation of books copied out by hand, volume giving birth to volume beneath the scratching quills of patient scribes. The rule of order in the scriptorium was absolute; Falconer Madan, keeper of manuscripts for Oxford at the turn of the last century, imagines the scene, where the rule of silence was so powerful that scribes used hand signals to indicate their needs:

> If a scribe needed a book, he extended his hands and made a movement as if turning over leaves. If it was a missal that he wanted, he super-added the sign of a cross; if a psalter, he placed his hands on his head in the shape of a crown (in reference to King David); if a lectionary, he pretended to wipe away the grease (which might have fallen on such a book from a candle). . . . Finally, if a pagan work was required, after the general sign, he scratched his ear in the manner of a dog!

Artificial light was strictly forbidden in the scriptorium, as the open flame of candles risked disaster in the presence of so many books. Thus writing for the monks, while central, was seasonal, restricted to the sunny months along with sowing, tending, and harvest.

The works the scribes copied were dictated by theology and monastic scholarship. The scribes were not authors but copyists—and yet this copying required a full measure of training and skill, a long apprenticeship to the severe tasks of transcription. But writing always invites invention: in an unbroken, onrushing stream of letterforms, there will be eddies and whirlpools, floods and freshets. Where medieval scribes found textual invention proscribed, they gave vent to enterprise in the art form that we call illumination. Madan evocatively imagines the evolution of decorative form in medieval manuscript writing:

> First, certain letters (usually the first letter of a new sentence, but sometimes the first letter of the line which *followed* the commencement of a sentence) were simply made larger than the rest, and perhaps coloured. Next, the ends and corners of such letters were exaggerated, and ran over into the margin, until in the course of time the whole margin was filled with offshoots from one or more large letters. At last the margin was formally separated from the letters, and received a wholly independent design. Meanwhile room was found either within a letter, or about a margin, or above the text, or on a separate page, for a miniature, the highest form of illumination, which in the best examples rivals in completeness and power the finest paintings of famous picture galleries.

Along with methods of decoration and illumination, scribal hands also proliferated. Styles of rough-and-ready handwriting first learned from Roman soldiers and notaries had been adapted to the strange vowels and guttural consonants of Northern Europe at the behest of abbots and feudal chiefs eager to keep the mysteries contained in letters secret. In centuries to come, amidst the warring, archipelagic polities of the early Middle Ages, the spidery forms of Merovingian, Visigothic, and Beneventan scripts would evolve among local fiefdoms and bishoprics—an efflorescence of variety meant to conceal meaning as much as express it. And thus for all the attention to the practices of copying—inarguably the dominant mode of literary practice in medieval Europe—error is rife throughout the European scribal record. Ironically, this erratic output is crucial to modern scholarship, as it often furnishes the chief means by which the genealogies of manuscripts may be measured. Scribes both produced errors and then faithfully reproduced them; copied and recopied, errors trace paths from one scriptorium to the next, connecting source to copy down through the Middle Ages.

The new scribal hand that emerged from Alcuin's school, Carolingian minuscule, combined the simple forms of late Roman script with the distinctive rhythm and grace of Insular hands (so named because they came from Alcuin's home in the British Isles). Alcuin and his scribes did much to clarify the scribal condition: they gave texts regularized punctuation and spacing, and introduced the use of capital letters to begin sentences and mark off major divisions in the text (they're not called uppercase and lowercase yet; those terms derive from printers' cases of metal type). Alcuin's scribes copied and commented upon thousands of works, and learning proliferated from the Pyrenees to the Danube. After twenty years of constant warfare, Charlemagne's pacified kingdom reorganized its energy in the form of learned pursuits. Alcuin's reforms reprise the civilizing mission of Charlemagne's reign in a lettered key—replacing proliferation with hierarchical order, ideals with standards, the whim of weather and seasons with steady accumulation; the forest for the garden.

A thousand years after Aeschylus and Euripides, Alcuin's scribes took up anew the work of writing libraries for medieval Europe.

Libraries aren't just collections of books; they're also totalizing statements, manifestos of graphic endurance, writing made powerful not through its expressiveness but by its prolix abundance, so ubiquitous it can afford to act no longer as mere transcription of utterance but as brick and stone, elemental stuff expanding to fill space. Yet at this seemingly imperial end point of what I mean by the magisterium of writing: its corpus-ness, its systematicity and unity, its seeming sufficiency and completeness—we discover another side to the enslaving power identified by Lévi-Strauss and Rousseau. For wherever writing seems to achieve preeminence as a tool of the powerful, we find at that moment that it becomes possible to take it apart and turn it upon itself, a line of that very same material quickened once more into a truth-making, universe-etching voice. This is what the Greek writers did as they transformed remembered tales into works of literature; it's what the scholars and writers and printers of early modern Europe would bequeath to us in the form of a republic of letters knitting those fragile strands of text into a web. It's what happens when we turn the rough tool for inscribing talents of gold and the exploits of kings into world-making, soul-changing verbal contraptions that reward innumerable readings, seemingly changeless prisms of written words capable of shifting and changing within us—in short, when we teach ourselves how to make literature.

An Alphabetic Sovereignty

Few authors' lives reveal the emancipatory potential of writing better than that of Charles Dickens, who wrote himself out of obscurity and poverty. From Dickens's fiction emerges the sense that writing is not only a positive personal and social quality to be fostered in good, progressive Victorian fashion; it is also a set of techniques for remaking the person, for fashioning a soul. It's a power that works on the author foremost and ripples outward through readers over time. This emancipatory power of writing is nowhere better demonstrated than in *Great Expectations*, where the silver thread of literacy is woven throughout the long account of Pip's travails.

For Pip, literacy is the Rubicon dividing innocence and experience. From the first lines, letters—these on his parents' gravestone—exert a lively influence upon his imagination. Pip can't read yet before his "first fancies regarding what they were like were unreasonably derived from their tombstones. The shape of the letters on my father's, gave me an odd idea that he was a square, stout, dark man, with curly black hair. From the character and turn of the inscription, 'Also Georgiana Wife of the Above,' I drew a childish conclusion that my mother was freckled and sickly." As Pip rows out upon the dark waters of literacy, it makes a change in him perceptible to his wise, unlettered stepfather, Joe:

> One night I was sitting in the chimney corner with my slate, expending great efforts on the production of a letter to Joe. I think it must have been a full year after our hunt upon the marshes, for it was a long time after, and it was winter and a hard frost. With an alphabet on the hearth at my feet for reference, I contrived in an hour or two to print and smear this epistle:—

> "MI DEER JO i OPE U R KR WITE WELL i OPE i SHAL SON B HABELL 4 2 TEEDGE U JO AN THEN WE SHORL B SO GLODD AN WEN i M

PRENGTD 2 U JO WOT LARX AN BLEVE ME INF
XN PIP."

There was no indispensable necessity for my communicating with Joe by letter, inasmuch as he sat beside me and we
were alone. But I delivered this written communication (slate
and all) with my own hand, and Joe received it as a miracle of
erudition.

"I say, Pip, old chap!" cried Joe, opening his blue eyes wide,
"what a scholar you are! An't you?"

Ignorant of letters himself, Joe takes naïve pride in Pip's lettering, and pronounces himself "uncommon fond" of reading: "'Give
me,' said Joe, 'a good book, or a good newspaper, and sit me down
afore a good fire, and I ask no better. Lord!' he continued, after
rubbing his knees a little, 'when you do come to a J and a O, and
says you, Here, at last, is a J-O, Joe, how interesting reading is!'"
Late in the novel, Joe produces a sensitive, utopian analysis of the
political economics of writing. For although literacy is challeng-
ing to acquire, it is not utterly beyond reach. "The king upon his
throne," he later tells Pip, "with his crown upon his ed, can't sit and
write his acts of Parliament in print, without having begun, when
he were a unpromoted Prince, with the alphabet." As far as Joe is
concerned, the alphabet is constitution enough; to him, the lad-
der of letters represents a ready means to class mobility—or more
fairly, a token of the equality of humankind.

It's striking the extent to which turning points throughout
Great Expectations arrive in the form of written documents. Late
in the book, when Pip's former patron and tormentor, Miss Havisham, offers to make amends for her past misuses by paying to

help set up Pip's close friend in business, she does so not by counting out fresh bills, but by making out a singular promissory note,
taking "from her pocket a yellow set of ivory tablets, mounted in
tarnished gold, and writing upon them with a pencil in a case of
tarnished gold that hung from her neck":

> She read me what she had written; and it was direct and clear,
> and evidently intended to absolve me from any suspicion of
> profiting by the receipt of the money. I took the tablets from
> her hand, and it trembled again, and it trembled more as she
> took off the chain to which the pencil was attached, and put
> it in mine. All this she did without looking at me.
>
> "My name is on the first leaf. If you can ever write under
> my name, 'I forgive her,' though ever so long after my broken
> heart is dust pray do it!"

The tormented Miss Havisham's ivory writing tablet is an ancient
technology. Tablets of wax were used in ancient times for ephemeral note-taking, and small notebooks like Miss Havisham's—
with erasable leaves of ivory, vellum, or washable, plaster-covered
paper—were important Renaissance accoutrements. Hamlet cites
such a notebook when contemplating his ghostly father's injunction to "remember me":

> *Remember thee?*
> *Yea, from the table of my memory*
> *I'll wipe away all trivial fond records,*
> *All saws of books, all forms, all pressures past,*
> *That youth and observation copied there*
> *And thy commandment all alone shall live*
> *Within the book and volume of my brain.*

Although such tablets were used into the nineteenth century, by Dickens's time they were rare. Miss Havisham's notebook is a throwback, another reminder of her will to bring time to a stop. Writing her remittance to Pip in such an unusual notebook is already a kind of promise: in their strangeness, the ivory leaves themselves are bond enough. It seems likely Dickens had Hamlet's "table of memory" in mind when he composed this image. Where Hamlet declares his father's injunction indelible, Miss Havisham would have Pip's forgiveness—a kind of erasure—inscribed upon her tablets, a revision of memory.

When Pip's old nemesis, Orlick, traps him in a sluice house on the marshes, planning to kill him, he reveals another side to writing. Like his former master, Pip's beloved Joe, Orlick is unlettered; but in place of innocence he practices a spite and envy that turn his illiteracy evil. He has befriended the forger Compeyson, whose false hyperliteracy he takes for truth. "I've took up with new companions, and new masters," he tells Pip. "Some of 'em writes my letters when I wants 'em wrote,—do you mind?—writes my letters, wolf! They writes fifty hands; they're not like sneaking you, as writes but one."

But when Pip escapes this and other scrapes, and is at last reunited with Joe, he finds that his faithful stepfather has learned to write:

At my own writing-table, pushed into a corner and cumbered with little bottles, Joe now sat down to his great work, first choosing a pen from the pen-tray as if it were a chest of large tools, and tucking up his sleeves as if he were going to wield a crow-bar or sledgehammer. It was necessary for Joe to hold on heavily to the table with his left elbow, and to get his right leg well out behind him, before he could begin; and when he did begin he made every down-stroke so slowly that it might have been six feet long, while at every up-stroke I could hear his pen spluttering extensively. He had a curious idea that the inkstand was on the side of him where it was not, and constantly dipped his pen into space, and seemed quite satisfied with the result. Occasionally, he was tripped up by some orthographical stumbling-block; but on the whole he got on very well indeed; and when he had signed his name, and had removed a finishing blot from the paper to the crown of his head with his two forefingers, he got up and hovered about the table, trying the effect of his performance from various points of view, as it lay there, with unbounded satisfaction.

Superficially, Joe's writing stance sounds clumsy and discomfited. In fact, Joe writes like an animal—and I mean that in a very particular way: with his leg thrown out and his intent head bowed, he writes hungrily, like a dog following a scent. In Joe, ultimately, we have Dickens's ideal of the writer: spluttering and blotting, gamely pursuing the letters' native truth, writing himself into a notable approximation of freedom.

But how is this graphic emancipation accomplished? Virginia Woolf offered a theory. "The only way for you to do it," she suggests in *A Room of One's Own*, "would be to talk of something else, looking steadily out of the window, and thus note, not with a pencil in a notebook, but in the shortest of shorthand, in words that are hardly syllabled yet, what happens when Olivia—this organism that has been under the shadow of the rock these million years—feels the light fall on it, and see coming her way a piece of strange food—knowledge, adventure, art. And she reaches out for it . . . and has to devise some entirely new combination of resources, so highly developed for other purposes, so as to absorb the new into the old without disturbing the intricate and elaborate balance of the whole."

While the passage above could serve as a useful description of the evolution of writing taken in its entirety, reordering and expanding the magisterium of writing to include women's consciousness is the subject of Woolf's great essay. By her time it had already been the work of generations, from Jane Austen and the Brontës to Margaret Fuller and Emily Dickinson to (the massively underappreciated) Sarah Orne Jewett, through Woolf herself and on to Maxine Kumin, Elizabeth Bishop, Clarice Lispector, Jeanette Winterson, and countless others—my list is far too short, and the work far from finished. In *A Room of One's Own*, Woolf charts how the seismic shifts of writing's place in human life not only operate on historical and geological time scales but also occur at the most intimate measures of individual observation and notation.

Like Lévi-Strauss, Woolf worries about libraries and their kingly, enslaving acquisitiveness, their remorseless discipline. At the beginning of *A Room of One's Own*, Woolf (in the person of the protagonist of this barbed and brilliant essay) has just attempted to follow a train of thought through the library doors at "Oxbridge." She hopes to examine a Milton manuscript mentioned in a stray quote, which, it seemed to her, might illustrate the fragile nature of just such trains of thought. Her way is blocked by a kindly old verger, however, who explains that women were not allowed in the library unless accompanied by a Fellow of the college or a letter of reference. Cursing demurely under her breath, the writer retreats.

"That a famous library has been cursed by a woman is a matter of complete indifference to a famous library," Woolf observes. "Venerable and calm, with all its treasures safe locked within its breast, it sleeps complacently and will, so far as I am concerned, so sleep for ever." A fragile, closely nurtured fancy has been injured by male privilege—a privilege by this point so ubiquitous and pro forma that a mere letter will do in place of an actual male chaperone. It's one thing to observe that a Fellow, necessarily male, would enjoy a standing not given to a woman; it's another thing to grant that same privilege to a written document, to give it a kind of surrogate masculine standing, implicitly measuring the weakness of the state in which woman, in the person of Woolf, finds herself when standing at the library door.

Throughout the history of writing, glyphs have been granted standing as objects, talismans, and tokens. Superficially, the powers and relations of written things seem to have a uniformly masculine character; from the clay-smudged scribes of the Fertile Crescent to the Chinese elite and their calligraphy examinations to Grub Street hacks who strove to colonize writing's provinces with all the rough vigor of a commoditized vernacular, writing has been overwhelmingly a male enterprise. But this doesn't tell us anything important about writing itself, except to remind us what Lévi-Strauss and Rousseau have already said—that it is born as an instrument of power. As such it suffers the gendered cramps and tensions of all such instruments. For Woolf teaches this as well: alongside writing's career as an instrumentality of power, it has pursued a flickering existence as a modality of consciousness. It's this career, I'd wager, that matters more to most of us in the end. And in this regard, writing has far to go in achieving anything like a full flowering. Writing's achievements are woven through with a yellow thread of injustice and alienation; pull it, and the whole thing unravels like a tawdry tapestry. But there is always new weaving to be done at the loom.

Woolf's contribution to the modes of literary invention is a staple of standardized tests. And yet it's not often remarked how thoroughly Woolf demonstrated that the putative "stream of con-sciousness" is born as a material thing: a stream of letters, a river of ink poured by hand and heart, subject to expropriation and alien-ation but slippery and alive. For Woolf (and, she shows, for the women of her time) this most ephemeral product finds its enemies even before it is committed to the page—in the sons and brothers who are chosen to receive the fine education, in the restrictions and proscriptions that guard the library door. Like other women writers before her, Woolf transformed those provinces of writing traditionally most open (or restricted) to women—the letter and the diary—into sumptuously productive sovereignties of inven-tion. But she explored further countries by bringing the material power of writing to bear upon ever more intimate (and previ-ously unassailable) regions—beyond conversation and the coun-terpoint of convention into the realms of consciousness itself, of all-but-incommunicably intimate modes of experience. Sallying forth into these undiscovered lands, she wins a kind of triumph *over* writing, a desegregation of writing's gendered magisterium. Her achievement of style is in fact one of substance, irrevocably transforming and expanding the possibilities of writing itself.

"Literature," writes poet and typographer Robert Bringhurst, "involves the use of language more for purposes of discovery than for purposes of control. It is a part of language itself: present, like language, in every human community. There are no natural lan-guages without stories, just as there are none without sentences. Yet literature is not the cause of writing. Literature in the written sense represents the triumph of language *over* writing: the subversion of writing for purposes that have little or nothing to do with social and economic control." In *A Room of One's Own*, Woolf shows us how that battle must be fought and won anew down through the generations—fought at windowsills and in bookstalls, at writing desks and in colleges. Woolf turned her back on the library that Oxbridge morning, but she did not leave it to sleep complacently. In her wake, the library was altered in all its arrangements.

The Importance of Question Marks

When Max Weinreich quipped about the condition of languages that lack armies, he was trying to explain the historic plight of Yiddish. Despite its long-standing lack of military and political power, Yiddish enjoys a rare standing in the family of languages. The literacy critic Harold Bloom, himself a native Yiddish-speaker, writes that "the language's curious wealth belies its apparent paucity of vocabulary." As in oral poetry, felicity and style in Yiddish are achieved through the skillful layering and countrapuntal handling of clusters of words, a technique that generates irony and allusiveness, ever renewing the flavor of the strange in the familiar. Surely the reasons for this are embedded in history itself, and not explicable by handy formulas. And just as surely, Yiddish's rich life as a written language plays a role. Walter J. Ong calls such a language a "grapholect": a "transdialectical language formed by deep commitment to writing." One of Ong's themes is the ramifying effect of writing upon the minds of literate speakers. Linearity, classification, all forms of "study" in its recognizable sense, as well as the awareness of vast archipelagos of words beyond one's immediate cognitive and expressive control, are some of the enriching endowments of literacy in Ong's reckoning.

The strength of Yiddish is that it is a double-walled fortress of writing's magisterium, a grapholect within grapholects. Written in Hebrew characters, Yiddish was defended from incursions of Germanic and Slavic languages that dominated the lands in which it was spoken. But Yiddish serves another grapholexical master: that of the Hebrew Torah. As Bloom puts it, it's a language that's always asking questions:

> The uncanny familiarity of Yiddish for Jewish (and some Gentile) nonspeakers has something to do with its insinuating, questioning quality. Yiddish is the Hamlet of languages; the Prince of Denmark's play abounds with questionable enigmas and a plethora of instances of the word "questions." . . . As illustrations I would suggest: "Why not?" "Why ask?" "Who asks?" "What is the alternative?" "What and how does it mean?" "If that is the case, then does not a question arise?" These all can be seen as deriving from the Talmud.

Open and inquiring, defended by its barbed, exotic orthography and the irony of its writers, Yiddish is an example par excellence of the unique powers and influences of writing's magisterium. Of course, in the end that's not enough, as Bloom points out. "Yiddish survived by its openness" to critique and commentary, he writes. "But no language can survive the destruction of the small children who had begun to speak it."

HOLY WRIT

To perceive the distance between the divine and the human, it is enough to compare these crude wavering symbols which my fallible hand scrawls on the cover of a book, with the organic characters inside: punctual, delicate, perfectly black, inimitably symmetrical.
—JORGE LUIS BORGES, "THE LIBRARY OF BABEL"

Bible Lessons

When it comes to the Bible, authorship is a hard notion to pin down. There is the Law, which takes for its materials stone and the fiery finger of God. Traditionally, authorship of the Torah (which in one view is an attribute or dimension of the divine) is attributed to Moses. But what is this writing with which Moses is credited? Under what conditions does it take place? Can we imagine Moses stopping to write amidst the straitened circumstances of the Exodus? The Qu'ran, like the Torah, is an aspect of God. Mohammed's encounter with writing is a vivid part of the Qu'ran itself: the Prophet's revelations over a period of twenty-three years were recited and memorized by the *sahaba*, Mohammed's acolyte army, who were ordered to learn how to write in order to record them. The word "Qu'ran" itself likely derives from the Syriac and Arabic words for "recitation" (Syriac *qeryana*, Arabic *qara'a*). "Torah," too, is a word meaning recitation or instruction.

The oral ingredients of scripture are everywhere apparent. The declamatory formulas of the Law found in the Torah; the fevered music of the Psalms and the Song of Solomon; the preacherly cadences of Jesus's sayings: the Bible is shot through with the texture of utterance—and yet utterance everywhere locked in embrace with writing. Unlike such ancient texts as the *Iliad* or *Gilgamesh*, writing in the Bible is not a ghostly presence, foreign and unreal, but woven into the book's great code. Proclamations, legislation, curse and denunciation . . . all are speech acts—but they're spoken to be written *as* spoken. Amidst the familiar tangle of proscriptions and prescriptions of the Law, rites both priestly and domestic, there is another subliminal ritual thread running throughout: the cycle of writing and recitation. It's a process with roots in the political culture of the Near East—specifically, in the treaties that suzerains impose upon their vassal lords. Such treaties followed a specific form, with preambles, a historical narrative enumerating the suzerain's many acts of beneficence on behalf of the vassal, a list of duties and expectations, the witness of divinities as well as the heavens and the earth, and an enumeration of blessings and curses that will flow from observance and transgression of the treaty's stipulations. As with legal proceedings to this day, the suzerainty treaties were equal parts ritual and written document; the reading out and delivery of the document was accompanied by various sacrifices and offerings.

As a tiny betwixt-and-between polity in the midst of the contentious Levant, Israel had ample opportunity to learn the legal expectations of suzerains, from the Hittites to the Persians to Alexander. Three times the Bible gives the Israelites' relationship with God the shape of vassalage, in the covenants of Noah, Abraham, and Moses; only in the last of these does the arrangement take written form explicitly in the narrative. In Exodus 19–25, Moses on Mount Sinai listens to God declaim the law, then he returns to the people at the foot of the mountain: this momentous dictation, complete with God's extraordinary, obsessive-compulsive design for his tabernacle, its furnishings, and the garments of his priests, Moses both recites and writes down: 24: 3-4, "Moses went down and repeated to the people all the words of the Lord, all his laws. With one voice the people answered, 'We will do everything the Lord has told us.' Moses wrote down all the words of the Lord."

The Sinai covenant, God's "treaty" with Israel, is based on precedent—specifically, those earlier, oral covenants made with Noah and Abraham, both of which take the form of ancient Near Eastern royal grants. Together, these agreements create a kind of case history of God's relationship with his people, a record of divine utterance taking on the texture of written documents. The documents are records, but they're also events—contracts, renewed through the unfolding narrative of the Bible, litigated by the oracles of the prophets. The magisterium of writing braids written words together with utterance, weaving itself into both daily life and the constitution of the world.

For all its constitutive force, the Bible is a strange document: divine, its omniscience is repetitive and self-contradictory; beyond authorship, it partakes of the selecting, privileging, and framing that are hallmarks of writerly activity. Ineluctably a written thing, it hides its own writing from us in a haze of myths and mystical formulae. It is, like the coat of young Joseph, one of its many serial protagonists and objects of its love, a thing of many colors and many

meanings. To the commentators of the Talmud, the Bible's multi-
tudes of meaning offered endless opportunities for contemplative
dispute; for mystics of the medieval Church, it is similarly a shim-
mering carpet of past lessons and future possibility; to modern lit-
eralists, its confounding quagmires reflect back to us only our own
incompleteness and imperfection. The distance between the tempo-
rary and imperfect and the blazing and eternal—like the difference
Jorge Luis Borges discerned between his own shaky script and the
symmetry of print—is the very gap writing seeks to bridge.

The literary critic Northrop Frye has a name for this
many-colored character of biblical meaning: he called it *polysemy*,
a word derived from the Greek to describe many-sided meaning.
The polysemous nature of the Bible, Frye avers, lends it an aspect—
which it shares with literature—of perpetual renewal. "One of the
commonest experiences of reading," Frye observes, "is the sense
of further discoveries to be made within the same structure of
words." This sense of reading was especially congenial to medieval readers, making the Middle Ages an era of textuality and polysemy, in which reading and writing interpenetrate. Frye quotes
Dante on the layered reading process of the medieval interpreter:
the meaning of a given work is not simple, Dante cautions, "but on
the contrary may be called polysemous, that is 'of more sense than
one'; for it is one sense which we get through the thing the letter
signifies; and the first is called literal, but the second allegorical
or mystic." To illustrate his point, Dante quotes from Psalms 114:
1–2: "When Israel came out of Egypt, and the house of Jacob from
a people of strange speech, Judaea became his sanctification, Israel
his power"; and he offers this explication of the passage's polysemy:
"For if we inspect the letter alone, the departure of the children
of Israel from Egypt in the time of Moses is presented to us; if the
allegory, our redemption wrought by Christ; if the moral sense,

the conversion of the soul from the grief and misery of sin to the state of grace is presented to us; if the anagogical, the departure of the holy soul from the slavery of this corruption to the liberty of eternal glory is presented to us."

Frye points out that this polysemy is not about different meanings, or even a "superimposed series of different contexts of understanding. . . . But different intensities or wider contexts of a continuous sense, unfolding like a plant out of a seed." Dante describes the four dimensions of medieval polysemy: the Literal, the Allegorical (which associates one set of acts and things with another), the Moral (where acts and things represent ethical choices and sketch the limits of right and wrong), and the Anagogical (in which the visible things of the phenomenal word stand like symbols—a kind of writing, in fact—for transcendent values).

It's a strict schemata, which tries to throw a cage over the Bible's full, feral range of possibility. This kind of polysemy is domesticated and controlled. Writing, however, in the Bible and throughout the magisterium, is a thing of shreds and patches, wonderfully wrought and figured. Between the universal and the polysemous, the bricolage of writing. Think of the turmoil of the Apocrypha, where the canon-making instinct is tripped up and confused. This turmoil—of canon-making and canon-breaking, but also of voice and place and ambiguity—is as essential to writing as pencil and pen. It is the very substance of the writing's encounter with the lived, the real—an encounter that results in the stuff we call text. Writing layers, it weaves, it jumbles, it confounds, it clarifies, it classifies, it collates, it effaces, it preserves. The effect is never one of ordering (although that is the ideology of many writing systems), but of interweaving. Writing is always palimpsestic; there is no setting-down that is not a setting-among, a setting-upon.

To trace the loops and whorls of unspooling meaning is a practice called *hermeneutics*, a word deriving from the Greek god Hermes. A messenger and a trickster, Hermes delighted in the strain felt by recipients in the parsing of divine missives—a strain recognized by the hermeneut, who in blind trust walks the path between sense and folly. The Christian practice of hermeneutics owes much to Jewish biblical exegesis, which developed an astonishing range of practices for the discovery of meaning in the Torah, including numerological calculations based on the number values of Hebrew letters, called *Gematria*, and the anagrammatical rearrangement of words, or *Notarikon*, as well as grammar, pronunciation, and logical deduction. Talmudic commentary takes its color and significance from its development as an oral engagement with the written law—a law that, primarily, is no mere list of instructions but is composed of an extraordinary entanglement of levels and senses.

Priests, Courtesans, and Plowed Wax

The entanglement mentioned above flows not only from the conveniences of interpretation but from the Bible's multimedia nature as well, its *longue-durée* welter of languages, scripts, and supports. Job's famous lament is one puzzling instance: "O that my words were now written! O that they were printed in a book!"(Job 19:23) This passage left many scribes scratching their heads. For what could Job mean by "printing" a millennium or more before the birth of Gutenberg? In the Latin of Saint Jerome, the relevant verbs are *scribantur* and *exarentur* (*quis mihi tribuat ut scribantur sermones mei quis mihi det ut exarentur in libro*). *Exarentur* comes from *exarare*, a verb frequently used in antiquity to mean "to note" or "to write," and frequently translated as "to print" by later writers. But its literal meaning to Latin readers and speakers of the ancient world was "to plow." This is no metaphor, however, but a simple descriptive term—for the ancients wrote most frequently not on paper or vellum or papyrus but by gouging their words into tablets of wax. Such tablets consisted of shallow panels of wood or ivory filled with beeswax and bound together into little booklets called *tabellae* or *pugillares* or sometimes *cerae* (pluralized "wax," here used as synecdoche). The literate used them as notebooks, or address books, and mobile devices—inscribing their thoughts and lists into them with a sturdy stylus made of bone or wood tipped with iron. *Exarare*, "to plow," describes perfectly the act of making marks in wax by gouging or scratching.

The wax tablet was the most common medium for writing from ancient times well into the Middle Ages, from the Near East and North Africa to western Europe. Ancient fresco portraits frequently depict their literate subjects holding wax tablet and stylus. By the seventeenth century, however, they were out of use, largely thanks to cheap paper. And as they were radically ephemeral, they disappeared almost entirely; very few examples of *tabellae* bearing writing exist today. Although the scribe who first wrote the words of Job knew no Latin, Jerome's meaning would have been perfectly comprehensible to him—for like the much-later Doctor of the Church, he would have been plowing words into wax. Throughout the Bible and much of ancient literature, writers deploy a rich vocabulary of metaphorical evocations of wax-tablet writing, bedeviling later translators to whom such flourishes were often incomprehensible.

Consider how the meanings of writing as task and labor might be expanded or transformed when wax tablets are in use: your hands and palms are oily, your words smudgy and angular. The beeswax is fragrant and smooth when freshly poured; once inscribed and reinscribed, rubbed out and darkened by candle soot, your text becomes a rippled, plowed-over field. But it's crucial to understand that these fields were not plowed alone. The business of writing in antiquity was still a labor that required many craftspeople to maintain. Saint Jerome is depicted in the extremity of solitude, a lonesome wilderness with only skulls and an inscrutable lion for company. But in fact his scholarly surroundings would have been busy with the work of scribes, stenographers, and amanuenses. In a letter to Augustine, he describes a dictational all-nighter he pulled, his secretaries furiously jotting down words by lamplight: "I dictated this letter, talking quickly, during one short night . . . wishing to show my detractors that I too could say the first thing that comes into my head . . . I extemporised as I spoke, and by the light of one small lamp poured forth my words in such profusion, that my tongue outstripped my secretaries' pens and my volubility baffled their shorthand tricks. I say this so that those who make no excuses for lack of ability may make some for lack of time."

It's a bit of a simplification to say that the Christian hermeneutics that emerged in the Middle Ages was comparatively simple and methodical—the literal-allegorical-moral-anagogical model so clearly demonstrated by Dante. The procedure has proven a conveniently flexible tool for wresting meaning from biblical passages despite the twists and turns of cultural and social change—a kind of biblical-historical shock absorber. But isn't this all about reading, not writing? No, it's about writing, too—for the ever-changing practices of the interpreters throughout the life of the Bible *have been part of its writing.* By testing the fitness of works for the canon, binding book to book through the connections of typology, allegory, and spiritual narrative, interpretation as much as revelation became the means of biblical authorship.

With the material and empirical expectations of the modern era, patience with the polysemous was strained. As the nineteenth century approached, a scientific notion of history based on sources

and verification framed the shortcomings of the Bible as a historical account. And so despite the pressure of orthodoxy, the unweaving of the Bible, like Newton's unweaving of the rainbow, began in
the seventeenth century, as thinkers began to question the pious
conceit of Moses's unique authorship. How could he have offered
firsthand descriptions of Palestine, a land God forbade him to
enter? How could he offer receipts from the history that transpired
after his own demise? Such questions were roundly condemned,
however, and authors who pondered them found their works
banned everywhere. In the mid-eighteenth century, French phy-
sician Jean Astruc systematically began to tabulate the discrepan-
cies and idiosyncrasies of the Torah. In particular he took notice
of the "doublets"—passages that told the same story or relayed
the same factoid, albeit in slightly different (and sometimes contradictory) detail. A striking pattern emerged: throughout these
doublets, God was almost invariably called JWHW in one and
Elohim in the other. In teasing out these doublets and comparing
them, further differences in style and detail could be discerned.
It seemed to Astruc as though the doublets were the residue of
multiple sources—and so he claimed in a 1757 book, published
anonymously, where he argued that the two strands represented
separate sources Moses used to recount tales he did not witness.
Astruc bent over backward to maintain Moses's position as unitary author; nonetheless, the cat was out of the bag: in place of the
traditional Mosaic theory, authorship in the Bible seemed to be a
true mosaic of different authors bent to different tasks.

Unweaving the story of Noah, for instance, the seeming contradictions and narrative missteps resolve into two separate tellings of
the same tale: one by the so-called Jahwist, known to scholars as J,
and another by E, or the Elohist. In the Bible as we know it—the
Bible as it has been known since roughly the fifth century BCE—

the separate strands are woven together into a composite: sometimes resonant, sometimes confusing—as when Noah looses first a bird that is first a dove and then a raven. Separated, the two strands come into focus as separate tellings of the same tale, with different emphases and shades of meaning—in J's version, God (called the LORD here in translation of the Jawhist's JWHW) is pensive and inclined to pity; the Elohist, meanwhile, has a documentarian's fascination with measures and dates.

There are darker and more telling differences as well. After leaving the ark, the Jahwist tells us (in Genesis 9:20–28), Noah plants a vineyard; "and he drank of the wine, and was drunken, and uncovered within his tent." His son Ham points out his foolishness to his two brothers, Shem and Japheth, who cover their father with a cloth. For his cruelty, Ham is cursed, and his descendants doomed to serve those of his brothers. Ham is the founder of Canaan; Shem (whose name is the basis of the word "Semitic") and Japheth are to rule over him. Thus the story of Noah's drunkenness, which belongs to J entirely, ties into ethnic and creedal differences that split the peoples of Palestine throughout ancient times. And everywhere J and E's differences are significant: J's stories privilege the peoples and traditions of Judea, the kingdom of southern Palestine after Solomon's time; the Elohist prefers the people and traditions of the northern kingdom, Israel. The two polities are part of the same tradition, the same faith, and the same people, albeit one with many strands, and differences of experience and opinion.

Using the method Astruc pioneered, nineteenth-century scholars ultimately identified no fewer than four separate sources— four different authors, essentially, whose works comprise what Jews call the Tanakh and Christians call the Old Testament. In the nineteenth century, a German scholar named Julius Wellhausen brought together insights from archaeological discoveries and increasingly sophisticated historical linguistics to create a complex picture of the Bible mosaic of authorship, now called the Documentary Hypothesis. Roughly, the picture looks like this: the Jahwist and the Elohist were roughly contemporary; they likely wrote in a script called paleo-Hebrew, derived late in the second millennium BCE from the Phoenician script, which arose in modern-day coastal Lebanon and would later spawn the Greek alphabet. Another author, the so-called Deuteronomist, wrote around 600 BCE, during a time of monarchical recentralization of religious law and practice, and he emphasized the tales that supported kingship and priestly authority deriving from the priests of Shiloh. A final author, the so-called P or Priestly author, whose stories celebrate the line of priests descending from Moses's brother Aaron. The four strands were likely brought together into a single Torah around 450 BCE, possibly by Ezra the Scribe, leader of the Jewish community during the Babylonian exile. During this time Jews in Babylon had adopted the Aramaic script, which also was derived from the Phoenician letters; their version of this script became the "square script" of the Hebrew alphabet we know today. Despite the plausibility and rigor of the Documentary Hypothesis, however, details of the source authors' identities remain shrouded. Some argue that the Priestly author may have been the prophet Jeremiah, by himself or in collaboration with Ezra the Scribe; Harold Bloom ascribes to the evocative theory that the Jahwist was an aristocratic woman of the court of Solomon, whose version of the story of Moses is in part an allegory for the lost splendors of the rule of King David.

Despite the central importance of writing in the development and practice of the faith, however, a Christian militancy against the word, against the book and the law and the learned, has asserted itself periodically throughout the history of the Church, gaining special force in Protestantism. Milton put it most clearly: "No passage of the Bible is to be interpreted in more than one sense." The polysemy of the medieval Church, however domesticating it tried to be, still observed the fruitful and feral diversity of the Bible. But latter-day biblical literalism presents another theory of writing: specifically of the univocal authorship of holy writ. Literalism imagines scripture as a voicing, as utterance—robbing it of the powers of writing in one stroke. In this view, the contradictions and confusions of biblical narrative stem not from the many braided streams out of which it flows but our own imperfection and temporal limitation. This suspicion of the complexity and interpretive uncertainty of writing has its roots in the teachings of Jesus, who shared some of the same displeasure with written things that animated Socrates. Where the Greek philosopher preferred to rely on dialogue to find the way to the right, Jesus hewed to the clarity of oral expression in sermon and parable to direct belief and action. Jesus's textual inscrutability points up a fascinating first-century ambivalence about writing—its role in a residually oral culture with a scriptural tradition—that would infiltrate the Christianity to come.

The ultimate justification for Jesus's reign, the deep-rooted proof of his identity, could be found only through creative readings of polysemous, saturnine, shifting symbols found in the Old Testament. Unlike his great missionary Paul, Jesus was no epistolator. And with Jesus, his whole insurrection, as it is shaped in the written Gospels, militates against a thing that *happens in writing*: most crucially, his offer of salvation stands as a rebuke of the written contract whose story is the chief drama of the Old Testament. In place of the written, graven law as bond and covenant he offers his flesh, his blood. And yet this is an attack mounted without explicit reference to writing. There is something Oedipal about it; in the divine confusion of the Trinity, Jesus's offer of self-sacrifice is also a negation of the Word in which his father was bodied forth. "In the beginning was the Word," says John 1:1; "and the Word was with God, and the Word was God." And there's the case of the story of the "woman taken in adultery" found in John 8:1–11, in which Jesus ostentatiously writes in the dust in answer to the charges of the scribes. Is this act a rebuke of the scribal vocation? It's been proposed that the episode takes place on the Sabbath, when writing is proscribed, although the law makes an allowance for writing in the earth. Thus it's argued that Jesus is showing his knowledge of the letter of the law, even as he prepares to call that letter into question. Furthermore, it's pointed out, his dust writing calls to mind a passage from Jeremiah 17:13, in which those who turn away from the Lord are warned that their names will be written in the dust.

I've already wondered whether there isn't something we might call Oedipal at work in Jesus's avoidance of writing. A corollary query in a mystical key: if the Word was with God, and the Word *was* God, does that make writing itself—the attempt to render a reliable image of utterance, of the word—a kind of idolatry? In *The Reasons of the Laws of Moses*, Maimonides discusses the problematic status of Egyptian hieroglyphics, which he sees as deified figures, idolatrous in nature. "It became absolutely necessary," he writes, "to prohibit stones with hieroglyphic inscriptions. Besides, in an age, where so great a propensity to superstition prevailed, stones with figures upon them, which the people could not understand, would have been a temptation to idolatry, even although the Egyptians had not deified them as they actually did." For Jesus of Nazareth, it seems, as for Socrates, the written word's variability was a quality of which he wished us to be wary.

Along with the other eschatological visionaries of his time, Jesus was reacting against many things: the blistering reign of Herod and his Roman overlords, the continued marginalization of the Jewish people, the seeming decadence of a belief in a polymorphous world.

Yet he was also reacting against writing itself—against its laws and proscriptions, its endless parsings and distinctions. It's ironic: for Christianity would take the magisterium of writing to new heights of complication and distress, and the followers of Jesus would trace their way in writings. Jesus's very immanence was a written thing; he was prefigured as much by the written avatars of the Tanakh as he was by the oral tradition—and after he departs the scene, the living practice of writing becomes the very cradle of his Church. To a remarkable extent, the spread of his faith surged through an epistolary network. These urgent conversations, which took place over years, lend to the New Testament their strange format, with intermediaries and lengthy intervals of silence during which feelings festered or grew clement.

The first and greatest of Jesus's saturnine explicators was Saul of Tarsus, who after an epiphany en route to Damascus becomes known as Paul. His tale is told in the Acts of the Apostles and some of the other spare, demotic narratives of the early Church. But it's in his own letters to the churches he founded that he explicates his vision of what followers of the Nazarene should believe and accomplish and expect in return. It's a striking aspect of the Christian Bible that such a large chunk of scripture is handed down as "letters," a newly risen island in the Bible's already strange and far-flung archipelago of forms and genres. Written in Koine Greek—a Mediterranean lingua franca that flourished in communities throughout the Roman world, pushed to the literary margins by the Latin of Juvenal and Martial, of Seneca and Pliny the Elder—these letters would be swiftly transformed by custom and belief into Holy Writ.

The early Christians led lives of enormous textual industry. The Bible at this time was a library unto itself, spanning Hebrew and the Greek of the Pentateuch, with books and chapters primitively bound in small notebooks, and many apocryphal and pseudepigraphic books vying for canonical status. The new faith inspired a florid explosion of sects and flavors, requiring would-be theologians to collect not only canonical texts but volumes of commentary and history, and even the works of the heresiarchs themselves, in order to edit, collate, and rebut them.

Paul, like all Christian figures, is frequently depicted by artists, and those depictions often have him writing. (Less frequently is writing depicted in the scriptures themselves.) Modern artists have favored an image of Paul after the image of Jerome: a solitary epistolator, sitting in contemplative attitude with scribal gear arrayed about him, studying in solitude some conundrum of faith in manuscript. The truth is different—for Paul too lived in a scribal age. Writing materials were expensive; secretaries and amanuenses were the norm; composition, for most writers, consisted of dictation. There are moments in the Epistles when scribal practice shows itself—take Galatians 6:11, where Paul says, "Look how big the letters are, now that I am writing to you in my own hand." It's as if he has taken over from a secretary to conclude this urgent, vituperative letter, wherein Paul sunders Christian practice from Jewish custom.

Conventionally, Paul's taking of pen in hand is treated as an attempt to affix a textual and scribal seal of authenticity to the letter—and (in the mention of the size of the letters) as evidence not only of his lack of practice with the pen, but perhaps his nearsightedness as well. But this moment in the letter also seems to be about Paul taking advantage of the unique authorial amplitude of scribal writing in the ancient world. An Epistle of Paul is no Romantic letter of comradely amity composed to overcome solitude and distance; it is instead a crowded space: composed in the presence of others, addressed not to a special sharer or unitary interlocutor but to an audience. And it's accompanied by a messenger—who is irreducibly part of the letter, authenticating it, offering witness and imprimatur-by-proxy. The author here dances behind a veil of choral fans, only to break through on occasion for a solo. He continues at 6:15, "Circumcision is nothing; uncircumcision is nothing; the only thing that counts is new creation!" Modern editions of the Bible interpolate the exclamation points; punctuation was not used in writing the demotic Greek of Paul's time. But for the faithful in Galatia, Paul supplied the exclamatory voice in the form of his own handwriting. "In future let no one make trouble for me," he scrawls in Galatians 6:17, "for I bear the marks of Jesus upon my body." Paul is writing of the scars he has received at the hands of the oppressors of the early Church; he's also implying, in the Bible's allusive, typological way, that his non-writing Lord has written upon him in letters even larger and more true, ever higher levels of autograph.

Beneath the pen of the Lord, Paul is like a piece of papyrus. And more—he is also the Lord's secretary, responsible for taking the divine dictation. In this way Paul recapitulates the prominence of secretaries and amanuenses—often slaves—in the writing practices of the ancient world. Some orthodox scholars have wanted to resist granting the secretarial dimension in Paul's letters, as it might seem to dilute his singular overmastering revelation. And yet as theologian E. Randolph Richards points out, the secretary's role was subsumed in a unique contrivance of the larger authorial role. Simply put, part of the ancient writer's job was to wrangle secretaries, to employ and master them, to bend them to one's voice and vision—author as the original *auteur*. If the author was the master, the secretaries were highly skilled supernumeraries. Scribal writing was not limited to penwork; ink and stylus needed to be prepared, papyrus procured or produced, notebooks and wax tablets cared for. The literate author was rarely possessed of the full panoply of writerly skills—and while most undoubtedly could write (mostly by scrawling in wax), they lacked the "practiced hand" by which papyrologists and epigraphers today readily distinguish the trained scribe from the literary pretender. Richards notes that Paul's work with his secretaries likely consisted of several revisions and queries, with the secretary in not only a clerical but an advisory or editorial role. On the other hand, many theologians (some of whom prefer the pious image of a dictation not given by Paul, but taken by him from the divine) argue that the difficulties of writing with papyrus and reed pen meant that revision would have been rare in the ancient world, too costly of time and materials. Indeed, our modern draft-and-revision habit of composition (now giving way to the infinite draft of writing on computers)—with sheets ripped from notepads or typewriters, balled up, and thrown into the waste can—has a distinctly modern stamp upon it.

But ancient scribes had other drafting tools at their disposal, such as the wax tablets described earlier, and even notebooks of polished parchment that could be marked and erased. Ancient authors such as Cicero would likely have used such media to rough out their thoughts, and would then turn over the notes to a secretary for polish and flow.

This much seems certain: Paul's secretaries were no street-corner scribes but skilled amanuenses versed in the epistolary conventions of the age. Paul's letters lack the intensity of classical allusiveness and rhetorical coloration of a Cicero or a Seneca but are fluent nonetheless.

The books of the New Testament are exceedingly murky in their origins, but they're united not only by their canonical enjambment and their subject matter but by language—specifically, the Koine Greek of the Hellenistic world in the Roman era. The residue of Alexander's conquests in the Near East, Koine's roots were ultimately in the Attic dialect of Athens, for millennia treated as the pinnacle of the tongue. But Koine evolved long after the emergence of writing in classical Greece, in a place and time far removed from the Athens of Plato and the playwrights, out of earshot of rhetorical debate and literary scholarship. The lack of classical allusion in the New Testament tells us much, not only about the personages of the early Church but about the authors and redactors who told their tales, and it reflects the alienation of rough-and-ready Koine from its highbrow Attic forerunner. For all the changes that had taken place, it emerged from the same sort of milieu—the market, the port, the city square, the public margins of empire—that had produced the Greek alphabet more than half a millennium before.

Archaeology furnishes clues from across the ancient Mediterranean world, from graffiti in Pompeii to the notes and letters of Roman soldiers in Britain. One of the greatest troves evincing the reach and significance of writing to ancient peoples is the vast treasury of discarded papyrus unearthed in the rubbish heaps of the ancient Egyptian city of Oxyrhynchus. Today, the town of el-Bahnasa covers the site of an ancient city that in its prime was the third largest in Hellenic Egypt, a regional capital watered by an extensive canal system. The canals also protected Oxyrhynchus from Nilotic floods that would have carried away refuse dumped at the edge of town, helping to preserve the discarded records of more than six centuries, from the dawn of Christianity to the time of the Arab invasion of Egypt.

Oxyrhynchus was missed in the early excavations carried out by nineteenth-century British Egyptologists—far up the Nile, its deposits largely consisting of rubbish mounds, it held little promise when compared to the glittering finds of the pyramids and the Valley of Kings. In the 1890s, two young Oxford archaeologists, Ben Grenfell and Arthur Hunt, realized the unique treasure of Oxyrhynchus: thousands of papyrus fragments representing an astonishing variety of writings: fragments of classical texts extant and previously unknown; early examples of the Septuagint, the Koine

Greek version of the Hebrew Bible made for the Alexandrian Jewish community; sources of gospels, letters, and books outside the Christian canon; lists of ingredients for potions and spells; marriage contracts, rental agreements, bills of debt, and hundreds of accounting, legal, and record-keeping documents. Taken together, they show how intimately writing was woven into every aspect of Hellenic life, touching both the genteel and the uneducated.

The fragmentary tragedy of Hypsipyle by Euripides, found in a fragment denoted as Oxy 852 in the notation system used by the scholarly editors of the papyri, is an example of the sort of material found in the archive. Previously known only from citations by ancient authors, Euripides's tale of the queen of Lemnos and the malodorous curse she earns from Aphrodite was pieced together from some two hundred flakes of papyrus. An accounting document on the back, consisting of numerals of Greek letters in a larger, crude hand, assisted a little in piecing the text together—and also attests to the reuse-and-recycle ethos of ancient scribal practice. Likely the text was prepared for reading or recitation; heavily corrected by another hand, it was abandoned, only to find new life as scratch paper for someone else. The text dates to about 200 CE.

Most Oxyrhynchus documents, however, are more everyday texts, revealing the warp and woof of ancient writing. Among the magical formulae are many that riff on the combinatorial properties of letters. "Great is the Lady Isis," begins Oxy 886. "The method is concerned with the 29 letters used by Hermes and Isis when searching for her brother and husband Osiris. Invoke the sun and all the gods in the deep concerning those things about which you wish to receive an omen. Take 29 leaves of a male palm, and inscribe on each of the leaves the names of the gods; then after a prayer lift them up two by two, and read that which is left at the last, and you will find wherein your omen consists, and you will obtain an illuminating answer." The modern editor of the Oxyrhynchus papyri was suitably suspicious of the fragment's claims, observing that "the scribe was a very illiterate person, and makes several mistakes" and noting drily that "as often happens with (esoteric) writings," this one purports "to be copied from a sacred book." Another fragment lists wrestling holds in "careful and rather large uncial writing," a sign of the writer's lack of scribal expertise. There are legal edicts and petitions, letters of appointment and declarations of birth—illuminating through writing the joints of life, so to speak—the many sorts of acts and relations dignified by the touch of writing in the daily life of an oasis and Roman outpost in the Greek Near East. The writers who sprang from this milieu shared tools and practices with their cultivated literary contemporaries, but little else. Cicero, for instance, who of course "wrote" in Latin, developed his ideas about rhetoric from Attic Greek exemplars far removed from the practical prose and staccato rhythms of Paul's Koine. His slave Tiro was a profoundly well-educated man who developed a form of shorthand and became an author in his own right when he won his freedom after Cicero's death. Cicero loved Tiro, but it was the love of a master for a slave.

The intimacy and social intensity of writing in the ancient world find their way into works of poets. Catullus, for instance, dramatizes literary writing as a ritual of friendship and shared purpose in his dedication of a collection of verse to his friend and patron, Cornelius:

> *To whom shall I give this pretty new treatise*
> *just polished with dry pumice?*
> *To you, Cornelius—for you used to be willing*
> *to think something of my scribbling.*

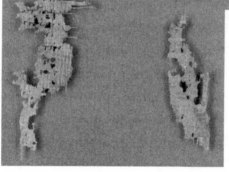

"Consider the ravens: They do not sow or reap, they have no storeroom or barn; yet God feeds them. . . . Consider how the lilies grow. They do not labor or spin. Yet I tell you, not even Solomon in all his splendor was dressed like one of these." These lines, from Luke 12, contain a cluster of phrases that can be traced back to "Q," the lost, postulated original source text for the Christian Gospels. In this fragment of papyrus, dating to the third century of the Common Era, the lilies are found without the ravens; differences in the wording here suggest that the phrasing is older than the version of Q that ends up in the canonical text of Luke. The possibilities raised by this fact are staggering: for the text in this fragment of papyrus is not Luke but the Gospel of Thomas, a noncanonical text long thought secondary. The papyrus itself was another fragment found at Oxyrhynchus in Egypt; its survival and careful preservation, with its sutures of Japanese paper and wheat paste, is as expressive as the words it contains—reminding us that, unlike the lilies, we labor and spin together over centuries and centuries.

Even as you alone sought in three stages
to explain the Italian ages:
learnèd, by Jove, and laborious!
Therefore take this little opus
for whatever it's worth, o patron muse—
may it last more than one generation of use.

There's much for us to savor in this delicious poem—and much that tells us about the scene of writing in the ancient world. We're in the presence of a unique object here—no fungible text fobbed off in multiple copies, but a singular expression taking the form of a unique keepsake. And the work has been "polished"— *expolitum*—with a pumice stone, a common step in the production of manuscripts on papyrus. This "polish" was a beloved trope of Catullus's, referring not only to the act of burnishing the page but to the perfection of literary expression as well—a formulation we retain to this day.

A generation later, the act of polishing is put to a different use by the scandalous, scatological poet Martial:

While my chapbook is new, its face yet unerased,
while the undried page still fears to be touched,
go, boy, and carry it as a gift to the dear friend
who merits my trifles foremost.
Now run, but wait—let's pair the book with a sponge:
these gifts of mine go together.
It's impossible, Faustinus, for many wipings
to salve our japes—but one wiping can.

Recalling Catullus, Martial, too, offers his manuscript as a friendly gift—but here the subtext is at once bawdier and more tender. In place of pumice, Martial plans to send along a sponge. It was a tool ancient writers used to erase newly inked letters—but sponges—affixed to sticks, and meant to be shared—were also furnished for purposes of intimate hygiene in public Roman toilets. Martial also evinces the provisional nature of the ancient written word, its predilection for palimpsestic erasure and reinvention: the manuscript on offer here is newly born, its ink still wet, and offered up on fresh papyrus with its face "as yet unerased"—a nod to the ancient practice of palimpsesting itself, of erasing, polishing, and reusing old sheets rather than putting expensive new leaves into play. The palimpsest here offers a piquant metaphor for a pleading Martial at poem's close: he's admitting that, while all he's done and said to hurt Faustinus in the past can't be fully erased, he hopes this offer of amity—in the form of a freshly written, unspoiled bouquet of verse—proves effective. As we know, the palimpsest never fully effaces what has been scribbled before but intimately puts new words into play with the old.

But if the written poems, inked and polished, are transferable as gift, the verses as spoken remain the poet's. For a poet of the manuscript world, it's not one's right to copy but to recite that must be defended:

News has it, Fidentinus, that my chapbooks
you recite to people as your own, unchanged.
If you want to call them mine, I will send my songs to you
   gratis;
If you call them your own, buy them, and yours they will be.

Martial is perhaps our first poet of intellectual property, a dogged defender of the rights that inhere in his work. It was in performance that a poet earned a living, winning patronage and forging the ties that would grant access to the tasteful—and the powerful. The poet will offer the poems for free, as long as credit is granted. But even here, the poet worries about the recitation of his *libellos*, the "little book" or chapbook—revealing the poem's essence as a thing made of written words. Martial was a master of this manuscript economy, at once starkly different from and hauntingly reminiscent of our own literary culture; in fact, the epigrammatist was the first to apply the word "plagiarist" to literature, using a Latin word for a kidnapper of slaves and youths to name a thief of the word:

> *I commend my works to you, Quintanus—*
> *if, that is, I can call them mine, the chapbooks*
> *which your poet recites.*
> *If they complain of their harsh usage,*
> *come, be their excellent advocate*
> *and, when that reciter calls himself their master,*
> *say that they are mine, set free.*
> *If this you will mention three or four times,*
> *you will lay this plagiarist to shame.*

Martial treats his poems as beloved servants sent forth into the world, only to find themselves beholden to a harsh, unknown master. Quintanus, a patron of this new master, is an attorney, and Martial challenges him to advocate for the poems that a reciter in his employ has taken as his own. Martial reminds him that he can liberate these poems in the same way a master makes a freeman of a slave in an act of manumission.

At the other end of the Roman world, Paul's letters hint at a far different social milieu from that of Cicero, Catullus, and Martial. From one side, there is the zeal of the new faith, and from the other the hint of a freewheeling tumble of mercantile life. Both put pressure on the elitism and master-slave hierarchy of Roman society. In his letters, Paul frequently mentions such followers as Titus and Timothy, who function as emissaries and collaborators. Paul's writing life both bears similarities to his aristocratic Roman contemporaries and exhibits striking differences as well.

Paul produced his letters in a shifting ecology of letter writing, where provenance and authenticity were both crucial and hard to verify. In 2 Thessalonians 2:2, Paul warns, "Do not suddenly lose your heads, do not be alarmed by any prophetic utterance, any pronouncement, or *any letter purporting to come from us* alleging that the day of the Lord is here" (my emphasis). Paul worries about the possibility of forgery (in a letter that is itself of doubtful authorship). There is a backdrop of discourse and controversy, of schism and debate, to the letters of Paul—of argument and foment couched in writing, referring to writing, shot through with writing. It's only part of the ecology of belief in the early Church, but Paul points to proclamations and prophecies as sources of error, of writing as a corrupt and imperfect mosaic. His attention is overrun with the work of interpreting signs, reading the present in terms of the past—but the doctrine, the faith itself, is springing forth in writing, bumping into writing, relating writing to speech and deed, writing that reads the past in signs and the future in wonders, writing writing itself into more writing, now and forever.

Writing by the Book

The striking thing about the Epistles is that they are radically incomplete—offering only brief glimpses of the lived texture of debate, oppression, fear, and evangelism comprising early Christian experience. Here and there they hint at a vital debate bodied forth in letters and utterances. But as an archive, the Epistles efface these competing views, offering only provisional traces, as any archive is apt to do. Writing, it is often said, offers complete and unbroken record keeping, the springboard of historical consciousness. But in fact it is its nature to create gaps, holes, lacunae. The earliest Pauline text extant, known as the Chester Beatty papyrus, is a gathering of ten letters dated to roughly 200 CE. One of the earliest collections of Christian manuscripts, it also includes portions of the Gospels, Acts, Revelations, and apocryphal books, as well as large sections of the Septuagint.

Unlike most texts of their time, the papyrus leaves of the Chester Beatty collections weren't scrolls; they were originally arranged into codices, or bound books: the form of the book we take for granted today, which was first taken up by Christians while the scroll still flourished among literate pagans. Throughout antiquity, a form of the codex had been used by Christian, Pagan, and Jew alike—not for reading, as we're accustomed to in the modern era but as notebooks for writing. Wax tablets were often bound along their edges into codex-like assemblages, and parchment leaves were bound into erasable booklets for note-taking as well. For reading texts, it was the scroll that ruled. Papyrus was especially easy to make into scrolls, because the fibers retained a bit of resinous pulp, which when moistened became sticky; thus prepared, the edges of papyrus sheets could be overlaid and pounded to combine them into a seamless whole. Writers didn't write on scrolls; they wrote on single sheets, which were later combined into scrolls. Moistening, pounding, and rolling—these were the means by which books were produced as objects in the ancient world, the means by which something written became something to be read.

The rise of the codex as an object to be read remains a mystery. The textual scholar T. C. Skeat argued that Christians adopted the codex because of its efficiency—a collection of the Gospels, matter for several scrolls, could be brought together in a single convenient bound volume. Others have conjectured that the codex's efficiency was first attractive to compilers of Paul's letters. It's a hair-splitting controversy, and one that's essentially insoluble; the earliest manuscripts, like the Chester Beatty papyri discussed above, contain both Epistles and Gospels, as well as Acts and Old Testament books. So many of the mysteries of the New Testament are artifacts of the writing economy: Paul's letters instance other letters, unknown and never collected; others seem to use, in efficient scribal fashion, fragments of boilerplate, the origins of which are also lost. There is a great deal of textual dark matter here—things written and lost, which still exert a pull on the prose.

The canon-making curation of Paul's letters may have worked against the preservation of these traces. With other ancient writers, such traces are often found at a remove: Cicero, for example, will mention needing a copy of one letter in another, describing the contents of lost correspondence, just as authors will cite works extant in their own time that have long since disappeared. For scholars, these fragmentary remarks and citations have spurred searches for lost text at least since the advent of Humanism in the fifteenth century. But Paul's letters were collected not as literature but as scripture—as self-sufficient revelation. What mattered to their first readers weren't their correspondences with other contemporary writings but with the Gospel stories—not yet collected as books in Paul's time but still an oral tradition of sayings and pericopes, or particles of narrative—and the multiple, interwoven meanings of the Bible played out in the acts of fickle Yahweh and the words of prophets, wanderers, and kings. The result looks like cherry-picking, but it's really the artifact of a mode of reading and writing that's native to the biblical mind.

There are vagrant clues here and there to Paul's use of the media of writing. In 2 Timothy 4:13, he laments his lonely and outcast state and asks his trusted friend to bring missing things, including his writings. 2 Timothy 4:9–13 transmits epistolary intimacies that are haunting—and as scripture very strange:

> *9* Do your best to join me soon. *10* Demas, his heart set on this present world, has deserted me and gone to Thessalonica; Crescens is away in Galatia; apart from Luke. *11* I have no one with me. Get hold of Mark and bring him with you; he is a great help to me. *12* Tychius I have sent to Ephesus. *13* When you come, bring the cloak I left with Carpus at Troas, and the books, particularly my notebooks.

Interestingly, scholars question the authenticity of the letters to Timothy, which fail to discuss points of theology that Paul held dear. Did some forger include this plaintive note at the end of 2 Timothy in order to mislead us?

Even if such were the case, the passage tells us that bound booklets in codex form were part of the scribal toolkit of Paul's time. There is little doubt that for Christians of Paul's time, the written word was a world of notebooks. Richards conjectures that the collection of Paul's letters was formed by Paul himself, kept in the "notebooks" referred to above for purposes of copying and record keeping. In this model, Paul's letters were in codex form from the very start. Paul was part of a generation of Christian writers practicing a new economy of writing and reading. Apostles, preachers, and the faithful were often scribally oriented migrants, carrying books of correspondence, notes, and texts copied down from their fellow believers.

The urge to share Paul's words must have been acute among these followers of Jesus—acute, and often furtive. They would have carried their precious notebooks, hurriedly copying into them new passages deemed fragments of the True Word. It's because of writing, not reading, that the codex becomes important to Christians, and ultimately becomes the world's dominant book form. In culture and society, language and literacy, history and sensibility, these argumentative, scribbling Christians differed greatly from the courtly authors and divine tale tellers who had woven together the Torah up to a millennium earlier. And yet their practices of creating and combining scriptural texts were at one level quite similar, even continuous, with those of the Jahwist and the Elohist. They used writing to make the legible past speak to a confusing present, caring more for the poetics of tradition, covenant, and revelation than the modern empirical specifics of history and authenticity. A community-building enterprise, their reading of history and the signs of God was also a writing, which created— in Old Testament and New—a text of such shifting and dazzling complexity and interdependence that it would serve as both the source and the uncanny example of the powers of writing for the generations that followed.

By the third century, Christian figures like Eusebius and his predecessor, Origen, were the custodians of large learned libraries. Their models for scribal monasticism would set in place patterns that would last millennia, as historians Anthony Grafton and Megan Williams have shown. Origen, who began his career as a teacher of Greek writing, sold off his books of literature when he took up his religious vocation. Origen's rejection of these works has traditionally been understood as emblematic of Christianity's wholesale abandonment of Greek literature; but as Grafton and Williams demonstrate, it was in fact a transition to other forms of writing. Origen was making room for a whole new range of works—not merely Christian books but philosophical ones as well. In his lifetime, Origen would write more than eight hundred works—a sizable ancient library in its own right. And he would have kept copies of those books close in order to produce copies for friends, students, and patrons, in the constant cycle of scribal reproduction that constituted publishing in the ancient world. The writing of those books was supported by a larger library of the works of other authors: Greek philosophers, including Plato and Pythagoras; histories like that written by Josephus of the Jewish uprisings of the time of Christ; commentary and exegesis of Hebrew scripture by Philo of Alexandria and other Jewish authorities; and the writings of critics and confreres in the burgeoning Church itself. With that vast collection of books came an array of scribal staff to produce and reproduce them. According to Eusebius, Origen enjoyed the support of shorthand secretaries to take dictation, scribes to turn those notes into polished prose, and young women trained in book hands to produce copies for his patrons. As with Paul, it helped to have a staff to be a prolific writer in the ancient world, and authorship was as much about managing human resources as it was about scholarship or well-balanced sentences.

Letters and Destinations

The world of new forms of writing, reading, and publishing by the early Christians laid the groundwork for modernity. Like the advent of the printing press twelve hundred years later, it appears today as a sudden transformation: before the Christians, scrolls and papyrus; after the rise of the Church, the codex and parchment. In fact (also like the emergence of the printed book), the transformation was slow and continual, spread out over a couple of centuries. But the ramifications of the change are no less significant.

It was by fomenting, supporting, and preserving further writing, as much as in their role as repositories of scripture, that books became important to the early Christians. Christianity arose in the Roman world against a backdrop of tremendous cultural turmoil and transformation. Greek philosophy was in the midst of a peculiar renascence, flowing into the empire from the Hellenic dynasties that had been founded by Alexander's successors in the Near East. In Alexandria in particular, Platonism had become infused with the esoteric flavor of mystery cults and ancient Egyptian lore. Schools vied with one another for students, patronage, and influence. Teachers sought to ground their legitimacy not only by claiming descent from other teachers but by amassing written troves of magical and ritual lore that could be combined with various flavors of philosophy. Thus connoisseurs of philosophy, who in earlier generations had been zealous guardians of particular traditions, became voracious collectors of esoterica. Where previously they sought the authentic and the pure, they now became open to the traditions of barbarian peoples as well—including the people of Palestine, with their gnosticism, their messianism, and their Christianity.

To the philosophers of Alexandria, writing retained the air of danger that had raised Socrates's suspicions. To a third-century figure like Plotinus, writing not only supplanted memory, it left one's ideas open to the uninformed attacks of others. It also made those ideas susceptible to being stolen by others; as publishers and record labels today are wary of the theft of their intellectual property, so the philosophers fretted over a piracy that might lead to the establishment of competitor schools. Thus they often guarded their teachings jealously, permitting only students long in their tutelage to take notes, make books, and pen commentaries. The bodies of written works that grew up around such schools were forests of cryptic commentary, masterpieces of misdirection, mystery cults of the written word. If the teaching of the magisterium of writing is openness, these libraries of the philosophers often prove that writing can be a kind of not-writing as well.

For the most part, however, the philosophical schools were hotbeds of textual innovation. Scribes developed precise and refined manuscript styles or hands, prescribed specialized means of laying out the scholarly texts of commentary and exegesis, and discovered a dozen and more subtle ways to make writing speak to writing. Seeking the authoritative words of school founders such as Epicurus or Zeno of Citium, philosophers sought scrolls in far-flung libraries and copied and collated the texts, combing for variations, which they catalogued and commented on in with great textual precision.

This, in the century following the time of Paul, was the milieu in which Christianity established itself. And in this upwelling of exotic ideas and febrile scholarly activity, early Christian leaders and scholars like Origen of Caesarea adapted the sophisticated techniques of the philosophical schools to their own, avowedly sectarian, ends. Later, however, as their orthodoxy stiffened, Christians saw Greek ideas as anathema—they would destroy Greek scrolls in libraries, helping to hasten the onset of the Dark Ages; and in Alexandria in 415, a mob attacked the great libraries, already in decline, and tore apart their defender Hypatia, a brilliant woman who was one of the last philosophers in the Hellenic tradition.

Writing, as Northrop Frye pointed out, is inherently polysemous—it's much more than "solid language"—more than utterance merely made visible, but an ever-proliferating forest of possible

Ostraca were the Post-it notes of the ancient world. To call them such catches a sense of their ubiquity in classical archaeology and a sense of their pedestrian utility as well, but it misses their strangeness to our time, their quiddity, their expressiveness of the rough and earthy contours of writing culture in antiquity. These shards of broken earthenware could carry shopping lists, curses, or personal messages, as does this fragment of a letter from the second century. They were used for balloting, typically premarked with characters signifying a candidate or issue and tossed by voters into ballot boxes of unbroken clay. When imagining the lettered cultures of the ancient world, which produced Ovid's Metamorphoses, the speeches of Cicero, and the Gospels, we must imagine not only the austerity of stone and the adhesiveness of papyrus but also the crack of the shattered pot, the scratch of calamus on clay.

meanings. In this sense the Bible doesn't merely function as a sourcebook for the monotheisms; through its collision of voices and modes, it extends and complicates the possibilities for writing. More than any other book, the Bible helps to create the world in which writing talks to writing through books and time. Through innumerable and anonymous acts of invention and contemplation taking place from the waning centuries of Mesopotamian power through the height of the Roman world, the law, the tales, and the poetry of the Bible were syllabled by countless pens and styluses. These choices were made to salve old wounds and fears, to cement bonds of community and identity, to hymn wisdom and truth, to express beauty and love and fear and terror. Letter by letter they took their place in a community of signs interacting in ceaseless combinatorial flux, presaging possible futures, shuffling useful pasts, rhyming hope with history.

The results are winding, confused, fraught with contradiction. In the moment of its writing, each letter, each character, each sign is a splitting, a cleaving-off, a fork in the road—between thought and expression, antecedent and consequent, paper and ink. Reading, the believer may try to resist this proliferation, practicing a literalism that makes war on polysemy at every turn. Or she may embrace it as the Bible's—and writing's—native idiom.

In the world of late antiquity in which the New Testament came into being, it can be confusing to speak of writing distinct from reading, of book distinct from notes, of authorship distinct from copying, editing, and commentary. "Publishing" as we think of it in the age of the printing press, as machinic mass-production, did not exist; every book was written out by hand. Each instance of book production was a reading and an editing; each book thus produced became a future exemplar for further copying. Although books were bought and sold, they were mostly gifted or lent, tokens in a gift economy in which texts acted as charged, individual presences, be they pumice-polished poetry or the fiery sentences of a prophet. A book given as a present today, by contrast, exists more or less as an end in itself: the act of giving invites reciprocation, but the book, whether read or not, likely ends up sitting on a shelf. The object signifies a connection to the republic of letters, to a public sphere considered in the abstract. The life of a book in late antiquity was livelier—given, to a scholar or an elite patron, it would be given into the care of a professional scribe or slave for copying; its presence would be noted in letters to like-minded friends and colleagues, who might send a slave to copy it or ask to borrow it. A library of such books was, like a modern library, "a means of storing cultural capital in material form," Grafton and Williams observe. "But in late antiquity that capital could much more readily be transformed into social capital than it is today, through the process of copying and dissemination." Such lending might be reciprocated with the gift or lending of other books.

Despite vast differences between ancient poets and the divines, their practices as readers and writers drew from a common stock of habits and norms. With Catullus, every ancient book offered an occasion not only for reading but for writing—copying, glossing, commenting, and letter-writing. For Martial and Paul alike, acts of writing produced not only books but also community, serving as social glue in the far-flung worlds of poets, philosophers, and scribes. A collection of books was thus a social network of writings and readings, of favors given and owed, of ideas held in common, of confraternities of thought and belief.

LOGOS
EX MACHINA

Writing Learns to Write

To the sixteenth-century English philosopher Francis Bacon, the scribal work reproduced below would seem a piece of practical magic, the materiality of applied science making a leap into the metaphysical: a piece of writing that, using nothing but ancient and recognizable glyphs, acts in concert with a sort of invisible machine to manufacture an endless stream of identical texts with their own invisible reproductive structure. Here is how it goes:

```
<script type="text/javascript">
var currDiv = $("#one");

var currPage = 1;

$(".nav").mouseenter(function() {
    if($(this).hasClass("active")) $(this).css("color",
"#FF1E00");
```

```
});

$(".nav").mouseleave(function() {
      if($(this).hasClass("active")) $(this).css("color",
"#000000");

});

$(".nav").click(function() {
      var searchNum;
      var id = $(this).attr("id");
      if($(this).hasClass("active")) {
            if(id=="prov") {
                  currDiv = $("#one");
                  $("#two").html("");
                  $("#three").html("");
                  $("#four").html("");
                  $("#five").html("");
                  zoomLevel = 0;
                  searchString = [];


            } else if(id== "collection") {
                  currDiv = $("#two");
                  $("#three").html("");
                  $("#four").html("");
                  $("#five").html("");
                  zoomLevel = 1;

            } else if(id=="format") {
                  currDiv = $("#three");
                  $("#four").html("");
                  $("#five").html("");
                  zoomLevel = 2;


            } else if(id == "objects") {
                  currDiv = $("#four");
                  $("#five").html("");
                  zoomLevel = 3;
```

```
			}
			$(this).nextAll(".nav").removeClass("active");
			$(this).nextAll(".path").html("blank").
	css("opacity", 0);

			$(".nav").removeClass("current");
			$(this).addClass("current");

			if(zoomLevel == 3) {
				$(currDiv).find("."+currPage).
	removeClass("hidden");
					$(".itemnav").removeClass("hidden");
					$(".hoverdiv").removeClass("hidden");
					if(currPage == 1) $("#loadless").
	addClass("hidden");
				}
				else $(currDiv).find("div").
	removeClass("hidden");
			$(currDiv).find("div").removeClass("active");

			for(i = 0; i < (searchString.length - zoomLevel);
	i++) {

				searchString.pop();
			}

		}

	});
```

It isn't magic, of course. It's code—in this case, an example of what's known as a high-level computer language, so called because its syntax specifies a high level of abstraction from the mathematical fundamentals of the machine language that pulses at computing's implacably austere heart. Reaching down through levels of deeper abstraction, computer code is a movable palimpsest, animated and articulate, the deeper layers of which undergird, energize, and enable the expressive surface.

A high-level language turns the elaborate logic needed to flip millions of switches off and on into mental objects we humans can intuit and grasp. Metaphor is the ineluctable idiom of modern computer programming, enabling it to yield software of the flexibility, power, and ubiquity to which we have grown accustomed. Its efficaciousness depends upon the interlacing of several layers of ever more arcane and machinic symbology, shepherding packets of information according to carefully modulated protocols of control, all quickened by the unstinting flow of electricity. Ultimately, however, these systems are actuated by text talking to text, logical symbols intertwined, the word immanent in ever more abstruse and withdrawn layers of hardware.

Computer code can deliver its expressive force and ramifying effects quite economically—indeed, even a single line of code, composed for systems and machines far simpler than those on our desktops today, can be a powerful mover of meaning, experience, and culture. One such line of code, rendered in the BASIC programming language, looks like this:

```
10 PRINT CHR$(205.5+RND(1)); : GOTO 10
```

At once simple and utterly inscrutable, this line of code is the topic of a recent book (which takes the line of code itself for its title) by poet and MIT professor Nick Montfort and a group of collaborators. Typed into a Commodore 64 computer of early 1980s vintage, this line of code causes the machine to "print" a torrent of / and \ characters to the computer's screen, producing a mosaic-like pattern of mesmerizing vitality. The craft of making variations on such patterns through subtle changes in the code, balancing economy of expression with intensity of effect, remains a popular creative outlet for some software developers to this day.

While code may seem neutral and merely instrumental, every element of the string of characters has its own cultural history. The command PRINT, for instance, doesn't cause a hard copy to be made, but to send a result to the screen for display—and yet it reflects the origins of BASIC as a programming language used on machines that employed teletype printers for display purposes, before glowing electronic screen became standard computing equipment. The string CHR$, a "function" in coding parlance, tells the computer to use what follows in parentheses to find and compute alphanumeric characters according to the ASCII encoding formula, which itself derives from the history of telegraphic communication. Montfort and his coauthors dive deeply into a close reading of this code, the systems on which it runs, and the precincts of design and technology practice in which its changes ring most resonantly. As Montfort's team writes,

> Code is a peculiar kind of text, written, maintained, and modified by programmers to make a machine operate. It is a text nonetheless, with many of the properties of more familiar documents. Code is not purely abstract and mathematical; it has significant social, political, and aesthetic dimensions. The way in which code connects to culture, affecting it and being influenced by it, can be traced by examining the specifics of programs by reading the code itself attentively.

Code is a kind of text that can't exist on its own. But what other kind of text has ever existed? Books argue their autonomy; letters and memos specify an occasion—and yet these things, as much as computer programs, exist in a shifting and dynamic network of other things, with writing at the heart of it all. Granted, computer software is writing of an especially elaborate sort, couched in particular systems of notation and fitted to highly specialized media that enable these magical eruptions and transpositions. Within the habitat of its specified discourse, this writing transforms itself and other programs—other writings—immediately, unfoldingly, of its own seeming accord. This is *writing that writes*. Writing that begins to act as if it knows itself. It's hard not to wonder whether *this*—software, programming, *code*, in short—is what writing has been striving to be from the very beginning.

The story of computing is often told as something that disrupts the magisterium of writing, an insurrection against the contemplative, ordered, reflective, human-centered, scholarly world of old. It's a pattern of thought most evidently expressed in the frequency with which we apply the formula "2.0"—derived from the versioning practices of those latter-day scribes, the programmers—to anything textured or tainted with digital technology. Education 2.0, the Library 2.0, Culture 2.0—such epithets have an intuitive punch. And yet they imply that there was only ever a version 1.0 of a given domain—*one* kind of school, *one* kind of book, *one* way of telling stories or making images or finding one's way over strange ground—before computers swarmed the scene. In fact, these things have been changing all along, oscillating around vital cores of habit and sentiment yet unfolding to reveal new patterns and arrangements in the swerve. An ever-changing magisterium of writing has indexed these changes and enabled them. So if we can see the ubiquity of computing in modern life not as an interruption or insurrection but as a renewal and renascence *of writing*—as above all another iteration of what writing *is* and *does*—a refreshing new take on information technology begins to open up.

In this panhistorical interweaving of writing and machinery— the *long* computer revolution, perhaps—we find the resources for the inventory of effects and occasions we call modernity. In every important way, the printed word—by which I mean writing made with movable type—is the first mass-produced material, made with the first industrially interchangeable parts. To understand computer code as reproductive, semiautonomous, quasi-conscious *writing* whose means are at the core of the information age, we have to go back much further than computers.

The Little Office of the Virgin

In a workshop in Bruges, the master illuminator and miniature painter Simon Bening is delicately applying luminous colors to a miniature illustration. His figures and tints are the last details to adorn a Book of Hours, the chief genre through which medieval lay readers interacted with sacred texts. It is April, and the northern light leaking in at the windows has a pale, wintry tint, in contrast to the midsummer hues of the miniature that seems to glow in the nimbus of Bening's foggy breath. The apprentice has laid out the frame in which the miniature is to appear alongside the text, sketched in the contours that Bening now bodies forth as soft green hills framed with flowering trees. His colors include the soft green of verdigris, made from copper filings, quicklime, and urine (preferably from boys); brittle yellows extracted from buckthorn berries mixed with alum; and for the richest customers, kermes red or St. John's Blood, from scale-insect larvae of the genus *Kermes* harvested from the roots of oaks on the saint's day, June 24. And of course there is silver and gold leaf to produce the flashes of light that gave the illuminator's craft its name.

The Book of Hours contained the Little Office of the Virgin, a cycle of prayers patterned on the rigorous schedule of devotions observed by members of religious orders from late antiquity to

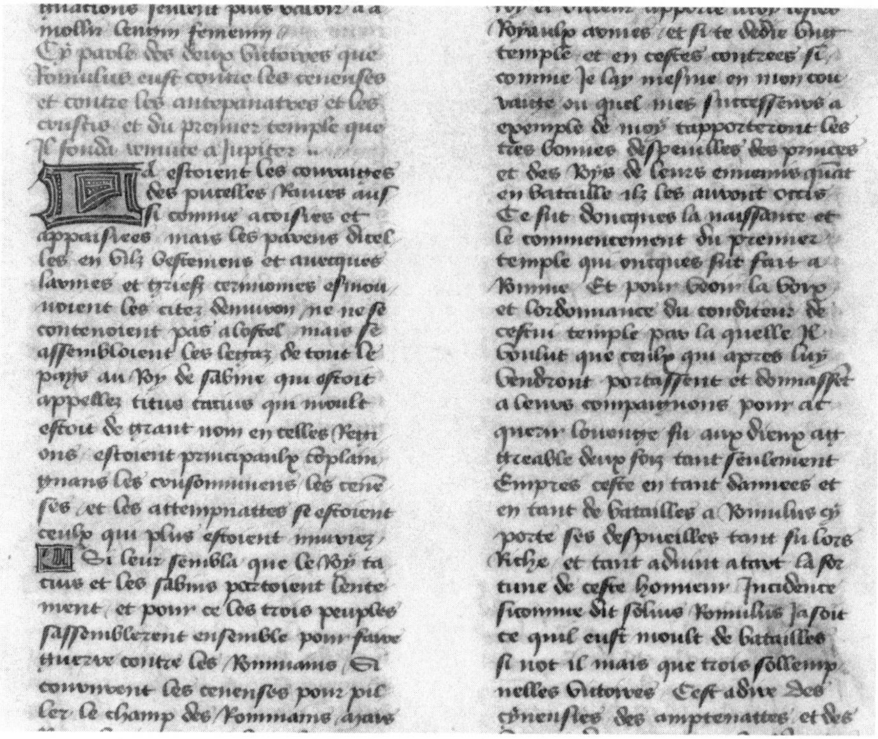

[Left manuscript — French cursive]

...nacions... pluis valour a a
molin... femenin...
Cy parle des deux histoires que
Romulus eust contre les ceninses
et contre les antepanates et des
... et du premier temple que
il fonda... a Jupiter...

[I]l estoient les communes
des pucelles... aussi
comme arrestees et
appaisees mais les parens d'icel-
les en... gesmens et avecques
larmes et triestes cerimonies esmou-
voient les citez. Environ ne se
contenoient pas a... mais se
assembloient les ceninses de tout le
pays au roy de sabine qui estoit
appellez titus tacius qui moult
estoit de grant nom en telles...
... estoient principaulx complai-
gnans les consommiens les cene-
ses et les attempnattes si estoient
ceulx qui plus estoient muviez.
[S]i leur sembla que le roy ta-
tius et les sabins partoient lente-
ment et pour ce les trois peuples
s'assemblerent ensemble pour faire
... contre les Romains. Si
comment les ceninses pour pil-
ler le champ des Romains...

[Right manuscript — French cursive]

roy... appellee...
... a vous et si te dedie ung
temple et en cestes contrees si
comme je l'ay... on... con-
vaine ou quel mes successeurs a
exemple de moy rapporteront les
tres grandes despeuilles des princes
et des roys et leurs ennemis quant
en bataille ilz les auront ocis.
Et si fut donnees la naissance et
le commencement du premier
temple qui onques fut fait a
Romme. Et pour donner la gloire
et l'ordonnance du conditeur de
cestui temple par laquelle il
voulut que ceulx qui apres luy
vendront portassent et donnassent
a leurs compaignons pour ac-
querir louenge si ung dieu...
... deux fois tant seulement
Empres ceste en tant d'armees et
en tant de batailles a Romulus em-
porte ses despueilles tant fu lors
riche et tant advint atant la fortune de cestui homme. En advience
si comme dit julius Romulus ja soit
ce qu'il eust moult de batailles
si n'ot il mais que trois sollemp-
nelles victoires. C'est adire des
ceninses des antepanates et des
...

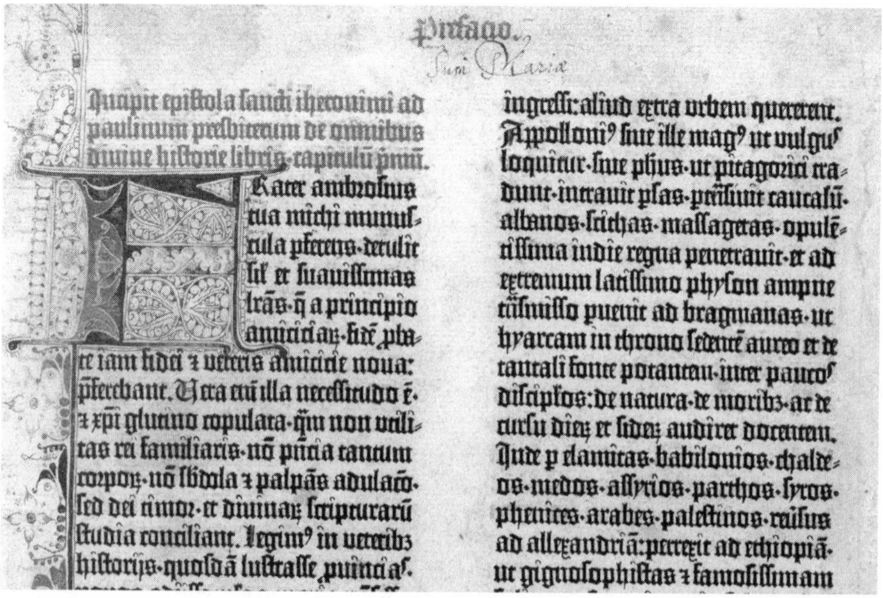

[Lower manuscript — Latin gothic (printed)]

Incipit epistola sancti iheronimi ad
paulinum presbiterum de omnibus
diuine historie libris. capitulu pmu.

[F]rater ambrosius
tua michi munus-
cula pferens detu-
lit simul et suauissimas
lras q̄ a principio
amicicias fide pba-
te iam fidei et veteris amicicie noua:
pferebant. Vera enim illa necessitudo e-
et xpi glutino copulata. quam non utili-
tas rei familiaris non pntia tantum
corpor nō subdola et palpas adulacio
sed dei timor et diuinar scripturarū
studia conciliant. legim in veteribz
historijs quosdam lustrasse puincias nouas
...

ingressi: aliud extra urbem quererent.
Apolloni9 siue ille mag9 ut uulgus
loquitur siue phus ut pitagorici tra-
dunt intrauit psas pertransiit caucasū
albanos scithas massagetas opule-
tissima indie regna penetrauit et ad
extremum latissimo physon amne
tāsmisso puenit ad bragmanas ut
hyarcam in throno sedentē aureo et de
tantali fonte potantem inter paucos
discipulos de natura de moribz ac de
cursu diē et sidē audiret docentē.
Inde p elamitas babilonios chalde-
os medos assyrios parthos syros
phenices arabes palestinos reuersus
ad alexandriā perrexit ad ethiopiā
ut gignosophistas et famosissimam

the present day. These books were immensely popular "tools of an all-pervasive individual devotion," in the words of bibliographer Nicolas Barker, "a part of the everyday existence of laity and religious alike." In addition to the daily round of prayers, Books of Hours were padded out with Gospel lessons and calendars; in sumptuously illuminated examples, illustrations were added to these sections to depict sacred and secular scenes. The standard cycle for the calendar consisted of the "Labors of the Months," a series of images of planting, harvesting, hunting, and merrymaking. The landscapes of the labors of the months were a particular specialty of Simon Bening, dean of the Guild of Saint John and Saint Luke in Bruges, the alliance of calligraphers, illuminators, and bookbinders in the late Middle Ages' greatest center for the production of Books of Hours. Bening would have painted his scenes after his fellow guild members, the calligraphers, had completed their work.

Bening and his colleagues in Bruges and Ghent produced the most spectacular Books of Hours known. But here's the astonishing part: Bening was born in 1483, some fifty years after Gutenberg first put his movable type to use in Mainz—today a four-hour drive across the German-Belgian border from Ghent. Bening's

FACING PAGE: These two pages span the disruption of the printing press: on the top, a leaf from a French manuscript text of Livy, produced in the first half of the fifteenth century; on the bottom, the forty-two-line Biblia Latina printed by Gutenberg at Mainz a few years later. What's striking here, despite the difference in letterforms, is the similarity between the two: in layout, in the disposition of text, and in decoration on the page, these two artifacts stand in continuity with each other. Gutenberg didn't seek to disrupt the scribal traditions of medieval Europe, but to participate in them, further them, and augment them. Writing, of course, finds its own ways in the world; although Socrates complained that writing never changes, never responds to conversation, it carries on its own conversation with us in deep time, changing its temper and our own in ever new and shifting ways.

work flourished in the first decades of the sixteenth century—at the same time that the printing press was working its wonders from Westminster to Constantinople.

Writing and the arts of the book had gone commercial long before the advent of movable type. By the middle of the twelfth century, the scribal arts were no longer cloistered but had developed into a secular industry—especially in Paris, where the concentration of ecclesiastical and scholarly institutions, at the head of which stood the theology faculty of the University of Paris, created an intense demand for bookish material. Manuscript books were still expensive—in the *Canterbury Tales*, Chaucer describes the Clerk as acquisitive only in the matter of books: "For hym was levere have at his beddes head/Twenty bookes, clad in blak or reed"; for these, he was willing to borrow money from his friends; "On bookes and on lernynge he it spente." In lectures and group study, the large, glossed Bible packed with learned commentary was the chief source, but scholars led varied lives of preaching and disputation, and needed smaller, less expensive texts to carry with them. An elaborate book trade grew up in Paris to rapidly and cheaply produce portable and even pocket-sized Bibles for this practical and transient trade—creating a new genre distinct from the ornate, massive, glossed lectern Bibles that were like the mainframe computers of the Middle Ages.

Out of dozens of parchmenters' and rubricators' and scribes' and binders' shops, a torrent of manuscript books flowed from the emergent demimonde of mercantile literati—an *avant la lettre* Grub Street who, according to thirteenth-century English philosopher Roger Bacon, expressed the twin faults of being "*illiterati et uxorati*": illiterate and married, and thus doubly transgressing the clerical boundaries set around the traditional scribe. Many of these were Bibles—the thirteenth-century's "Paris Bible," the name given to small, cheap editions of the holy book, tailored to the student market. Books for thirteenth-century students in Paris and the Italian universities were available as "peciae," typically four-leaf excerpted sections of lengthy works that could be purchased and shared or even rented from stationers' shops. And these shops produced a host of inexpensive books on sacred and secular topics—parables and fables, lives of saints and idylls of knights, books of hours and tales of courtly love—which already exhibited characteristics of the literary marketplace that would spread throughout Europe two centuries later in the context of the press.

That Marvelous Man

Throughout the first decades of the print era, the habits of manuscript making and use still mattered to scholars; the copying out of books was an important part of their scholarly as well as their mercantile consumption. Early printed books featured decorated initials and many other design elements derived from manuscript books; additionally, readers often found it more expeditious to borrow printed books and have them copied out than go to the trouble of finding a bookseller with multiple copies of the same edition on hand. Vespasiano da Bisticci, the fifteenth-century bookseller to the duke of Urbino and many other elite patrons, famously declined to deal in printed books—but the manuscripts his scribes made for the duke and other clients likely were copied from printed books in many cases. The reason was straightforward enough: if manuscript books were rare and costly before printing arrived, after its advent they remained so. And yet the interests of collectors would hardly exhaust the symbiotic relationship of manuscript and the press in scholarly discipline.

In the first century or so after the introduction of movable type, printers themselves were intensely interested in the origins and history of their craft. But in modern times, the transformative effect of print was largely taken for granted by the historians of the Renaissance. This began to change in the mid-twentieth century with the publication of historian Elizabeth Eisenstein's monumental *The Printing Press as an Agent of Change*, which charted the transformations in habits of work and mind that took place in the context of the diffusion of movable type throughout Europe in the early modern era. Eisenstein's research took place in the midst of the great efflorescence of media technologies, with the impact of radio, television, and telecommunications widely observed and debated. By way of analogy to these consciousness-transforming effects, Eisenstein charted the trajectory of manifold transformations in the intellectual and cultural occasions of writing in the West: the duplication of figures and designs; the rigorous, documentable progress of new editions and other textual transformations; the stricter periodization of historical phenomena; the tabulation of data and collation of text—all of these lend crucial flavors to the stew of modernity.

The nature of this change is hard to pin down: the increase in the sheer number of books, the rapidity with which they could be produced, and the accuracy with which they could be printed all appear as startling transformations in the magisterium of writing. But the press appeared in different forms in different parts of Europe, answering to different constituencies of authors, craft and mercantile guilds, and political and ecclesiastical authorities. Movable type introduced a new layer of material transformation into the process of making language visible and durable, and the world of writers and readers struggled to reformulate concepts of authorship, ownership, and truth in its light. The effects were nowhere so clean-cut and consequential as they seem in retrospect today, when new digital technologies seem nearly daily to sweep through our lives, promising revolutionary change. It's clear, however, that the printing press furthered a series of swift transformations in the very form and physical nature of writing itself, making the word the first machine-made, mass-produced material in history.

Scripts of the fifteenth century came in a wide variety of styles, having emerged from monasteries widely separated by the fragmented political geography of medieval Europe to suit different needs and occasions. They can be grouped into types: *textura*, *rotunda*, and *batarde*. Heavy and angular, the textura hand, which we think of as blackletter, Gothic, or pointed letters, was used in Bibles and liturgical books. Rotunda looked more like the roman letters of today; it shows up most frequently in scholarly works. Batarde was riotously diverse, a cursive family whose denizens remind modern readers of italic—which indeed is a species of batarde. It found its way into secular books, and it was the daily hand of business and governmental affairs.

From a certain perspective, the advent of the press looks like the death of writing—the end of the manuscript as the dominant mode of recording, managing, conveying, and archiving discourse in written form. In sheer quantity, printed works swiftly overwhelmed books in manuscript; by the end of the fifteenth century, more books had been printed than had been produced in Europe throughout the entire Middle Ages. And the qualities of these works differed vastly from those in manuscript. From our accustomed angle, it looks as though with the rise of print the scribal world found itself in eclipse, and an entire way of life winked out, giving way at once before the onrushing machine. Yet as we've seen, the craft and technology of the press didn't so much erase the scribal arts as incorporate them. The intimate, artisanal, cognitively rich round of scribal craft—the preparation of vellum and parchment from hides; the mixing of inks and pigments; the pounding and pouncing and rubricating and illuminating and the slow penning of dusky, barbed letters, one at a time—dissolved by slow degrees in a rising sea of ink.

Of course, the reality is more nuanced and complex. For the printed word is irreducibly a written word. Type bears the traces of the scribal hand as well as the marks of the metalsmith, the punch cutter, the machinist. And deeper traces may be discerned as well—for in the crafting of printed letters the type designers excavated ancient styles, fashions, and embellishments that had been discarded over the scribal centuries, putting some of the graphic tricks of antiquity developed for carving letters in stone to refreshed use in the context of movable type. A printed letter of the late fifteenth century is a mélange and an archaeological site where ancient iconography, medieval expressiveness, and machine-age efficiencies mingle. Indeed the modern flexibility of type is fundamentally based in this archaeological character; the printer mixes the means and modes of many eras to produce the efficient, modulated, expressive qualities of typographical style.

Let's look at some printed letters and unwind a few of their evolved, commingled traits:

S   P   Q   R

The legend above is set in a typeface called Trajan (and by the way, these species of type, Trajan as well as the more familiar sorts, from Times New Roman to Helvetica, are traditionally called *typefaces* or *faces*; *font* describes the size of the particular type). A message found carved in stone throughout Rome, it stands for Senatus Populusque Romanus, or "the Senate and People of Rome." It is the formula for the Roman republic, expressed in letters that have taken this graphic form from Augustus's time down to the present day (it is still found on the sewer grates and fountains that are the ancients' most ubiquitous endowments to modern Rome). Trajan, the typeface used on the previous page, is a modern face based on the characters inscribed in Trajan's column, a remarkable monument to the emperor's conquest of the Dacians, a tribe occupying a region east of the Danube River from contemporary Romania to Ukraine. The stems and bowls of these capitals are modulated—they vary in thickness, in a pattern that is predictable, with thickened, waterfall-like verticals out of which thinner horizontals seem to trickle and spread. These are the necessary embellishments of the brush used by Roman scribes to paint the letters in ink on marble surfaces for the ringing excavation of the stonecutter's chisel—an affordance that the Italian humanist scribes sought to emulate with their quills and nibs. The serifs, too, figure the rounding-off of brushstrokes, a reflexive maneuver made to give each letter its distinctiveness and independence from other characters—although in the case of the *Q* and the *R*, these serifs also trail off to the right in cursive invitations to the line of letters to come. In the chiseling, serifs make a subtle transformation from the flourish of boar-hair brush or feather quill to the sharp solidity of hammer and whetted blade—a keenness recovered by the type designers, who cut letters for the mold with chisels and punches, recapitulating at tiny scale, with the goldsmith's tool kit, the features shaped by ringing hammers and Roman sweat. The serifs give these capitals their foundations, lend them an architectural stability and strength, a pattern language upon which our reading eyes have come to rely.

Where the letters are carved, they also carve: the apertures or open spaces within and between the letters not only convey meaning but contain traces of their history as well. There is the rhyming equivalence of interior spaces in the P and the R, those kidney-shaped lozenges staring out at us, improbably balanced eggs and bowls turned on edge. In the Trajan capital face these apertures are subtly different; that of the P is left open, the bottom of its belly unattached, admitting a bit of white as if to communicate with the broader world. But in most printed letters, these apertures express more systematic affinities, as we can see if we introduce their lowercase analogues into the mix. Let's take just the middle characters in the legend on page 168 and make them small:

p q

We're already in the midst of typographical lore here—for in the *p* and the *q* we have a mirrored set, which in the context of movable type is both small and reversed with respect to the direction of reading. But the minor headache of keeping *p*'s and *q*'s separate was offset by a tremendous and subtle efficiency: the apertures of these two letters can be made identical (in some typefaces, each character is a mirror image of the other). For the type cutter, this means that they can both be created with a stroke of the same tool, called a counterpunch. Making and using the counterpunch begins the process of fashioning the end of a fine piece of hardened tool steel into the shape of a letter. The resulting tool is called a punch, and its invention preceded that of print; punches were used to strike tiny letters into leather and silver, and had even been used sporadically throughout the late Middle Ages to print individual letters onto paper or parchment. Gutenberg was not a scribe or cleric, but a member of the goldsmiths' guild; perhaps his crucial innovation was to turn the goldsmiths' punches into the basis of a process by which many identical letters could be made.

To create a typographical letter *q*, the type cutter begins with a small metal blank and strikes into it with a counterpunch, the tip of which is honed to the shape of the interior cavity of the *p* and the *q*—and of course the same shape, as the punch cutters realized, could be made to serve in the production of *b* and *d* as well. Around the depression thus conceived, the punch cutter proceeds to carve the stems and serifs of the letter using very fine files and gravers to dig or grate off vanishingly small bits of metal. The resulting punch of the whole letter is struck into a soft metal matrix, which serves as the basis of a mold into which hot-type metal—a mixture of tin, antimony, and lead—is poured. The ingredients of this alloy comprise a formula thought to have been settled upon by the goldsmith Johannes Gutenberg, combining the supple softness of lead with the durability of tin; the antimony—which, like water, expands as it cools—stops the molten metal from shrinking and distorting as it hardens.

These metallurgical properties were discovered by the alchemists well before Gutenberg's time; his novelty consisted in turning their speculative work toward the practical task of mass production. The resulting metal letters are hybrid creatures, "writing" that could in no recognizable way be written. The type designer Fred Smeijers makes a distinction among three kinds of letters: those that are written, those that are drawn, and those that are typographically reproduced. Written letters are the product of scribe and scribbler alike, produced in running lines of pencil, pen, charcoal, or crayon. The text of medieval manuscripts and modern grocery lists—until Gutenberg, the vast majority (though not all) letters ever produced—are made by writing, according to Smeijer's narrow definition. Drawn letters, by contrast, are elaborated, outlined and filled in or pieced together out of many strokes of the pen; such are the works of sign painters and artists, and the historiated, rubricated, and illuminated initials of medieval manuscripts. Finally, the esoteric, manifold production of letters by typographic machines manufactured letters that hide, rather than reveal, their means of production.

The first punch cutters and type designers turned to the scribes for letterforms, adapting them to the qualities of carved and molten metal in the context of mechanical production. Gutenberg and his early colleagues worked with the gothic writing with which they were most familiar. These letterforms had already become highly stylized to optimize scribal reproduction of manuscripts. Although they look ornate to our eyes, gothic letters are simple configurations of a small set of repeatable pen strokes:

i n m

With the Gutenberg Bible and other early German printed books, the punch cutters and typographers sought to reproduce those gothic forms as closely as possible, not merely in order to copy them and thus compete with scribal reproduction in the marketplace but because they comprised the books they knew and read—and were already highly refined, simple, and repeatable. The scribal hands of the late Middle Ages made up a mature technology, richly specified for a vast spectrum of uses; seen from the vantage point of fifteenth-century Bruges, there was no reason to hope for better. But as printing spread south into Italy, printers turned to a new source for letters: the Renaissance humanists, whose scribal inventions by the fifteenth century were following a much different path from that of their colleagues to the north.

In search of the blend of novelty and antiquity that characterizes the Renaissance mind, humanists refashioned letters by looking to the deep past. Much of the impetus came from Petrarch: writing a full century before the advent of the press, the poet celebrated the letters he found in Carolingian manuscripts, which, along with contemporary authorities, he believed had been penned by the amanuenses of ancient Rome. They took these scraps and folios to be the manuscript leavings of ancient Greeks and Romans, but in fact they were the work of Carolingian scribes of that earlier renascence: the simple, linear letters created by Alcuin's scribes in the court of Charlemagne. However, the typographers looked not only to the page but also to the walls, to the monumental Roman ruins that littered the landscape. From these they took their majuscules, the square-limbed capitals inscribed on foundation stones and triumphal arches, and adapted the bipedal-looking serifs they found on the Roman capitals to all the letters, big and small, giving them a flowing, unified character. The result was a hybrid alphabet of big and small letters, which the printers later would sort into upper and lower "cases" of type. The light, deft humanist hand that resulted strongly contrasted with the heavy black letters of the gothic; although inspired by an imagined past, these letters came to figure and typify the modern. And yet for all their modernity, the humanist styles were written things: handcrafted, unique, bearing the traces of their scribal past.

In adapting these Petrarchan letters, typographers introduced machinic efficiencies through reusable counterpunches, their rigorously measured qualities of fonts in body or x-height, ascenders, and descenders. Producing small bits of type metal with precise, justified, clean-printing letters on them entails a number of steps that combine scribal design with metalwork and machining; the letterforms that result are hybrid characters bearing the traces of Rome, humanist scribes, and Gutenberg's colleagues in the guilds of smiths.

However gradually the reign of print emerged, there can be no doubt that movable type had a galvanizing impact on the European imagination from the start. In 1455 the future Pope Pius

II wrote to Cardinal Juan Carvajal about pages of the new Bible
he had recently seen—the forty-two-line Bible printed in Mainz,
commonly known as the Gutenberg Bible:

> Of that marvelous man seen at Frankfurt, nothing that
> was written to me is false. I have not seen complete Bibles,
> but only some quires of various books (of the Bible), their
> lettering most clean and correct, nowhere deceptive, which
> your grace would read without effort, and indeed without
> glasses. . . . I fear it won't be possible [to return and pur-
> chase a copy], both because of the length of the journey and
> because buyers were said to be lined up before the volumes
> were finished.

Writing as Enea Silvio Piccolomini, the future pope had been sent
to preside over the Diet of Frankfurt, where a presentation was
offered on a project, then still incomplete, to produce a Bible by
mechanical means. What Piccolomini saw was not even the finished product but a sort of beta test: printed sheets that had been
folded into groups called quires or signatures, to be bound together
into finished volumes. But the prospects for the project—indicated
in the clarity and correctness of the letters themselves—clearly
impressed the future pope. The commercial success of the venture
seemed assured already, the prospects for its author bright—and
yet the "marvelous" figure who started it remains veiled: It's not
even clear whether Piccolomini himself saw Gutenberg, or merely
heard a report of the presentation secondhand—or even whether it
was Gutenberg who was seen; it may have been one of Gutenberg's
partners, Fust or Schöffer, who would take his printing business
from him amidst the chaos of bankruptcy.

We often treat the Gutenberg Bible as if it arrived as miraculously as Piccolomini describes it: dropping fully formed from the brow of Johannes, a finished, printed book like those we know and love today; it might as well have had a dust jacket, blurbs, and an ISBN barcode. But in fact the Gutenberg Bibles (no two he produced are identical), like most printed books produced in the fifteenth and sixteenth centuries, were hybrid affairs, combining the tried-and-true means of pen, ink, and paint with the reproductive power of the press. Like many printed books that followed in the years it took for printing to spread throughout Europe, the pages of Gutenberg's Bible were laid out with empty spaces for decorated initials, page numbers, and rubrications—red-lettered text—to guide the reader. Well into the sixteenth century, printed books were produced with space in the margins for custom-painted borders and added illustrations. Far from putting the scribes and illuminators of the late Middle Ages out of work, the technology of the press offered these artisans a new medium and new markets for the labor.

Of the supposed author of this disruptive and ungovernable technology, so little may be said. Substantial data from the life of Johannes Gutenberg eluded the fine-meshed net of printed words; the details that come down to us are scanty and few. His background was mercantile and bourgeois; his family rose to prosperity in the modern context of a chartered town whose citizens were given leave by their prince to govern their own affairs. He was a member of the goldsmiths' guild: the early modern guilds combined the latter-day affordances of the labor union, the Rotary Club, and the Chamber of Commerce, and we don't know whether Gutenberg's guild membership signifies a master craftsman or a dealer in new and used goods. This much is clear, however: Gutenberg hails from the bourgeois, a townsman and constituent of a newly dignified class of artisans and merchants. Neither a scholar nor a divine, Gutenberg meshes cultural aspiration with practical acumen in a way we've come to know as middle-class.

Whatever his brilliance as a smith, machinist, and inventor, his name nearly escaped the pages of history altogether. His partners, the banker Johann Fust and the scribe Peter Schöffer, fleeced him in a lawsuit, ending up the proprietors of Gutenberg's press. Fust was an evangelist for the medium, giving many demonstrations of its powers, such as the one to which Piccolomini alluded in his letter to Cardinal Carvajal. Fust, whose name was sometimes spelled Faust, was evidently a persuasive performer of the magical powers of the press; some versions of the Faust legend seem to take cues from his life. Schöffer, meanwhile, became one of the most prolific of the first generation of printers. Later accounts would argue for the primacy of Fust or Schöffer over that of Gutenberg; the truth seems lost to record, print or manuscript. The Gutenberg Bibles have been subjected to the most intense scrutiny of perhaps any book in existence, and yet the working methods of Gutenberg's shop are still not entirely clear. But it's certain that thanks to Fust's business sense and the sheer skill of Schöffer, printing with movable type swiftly spread to all corners of Europe—even (and especially) to those last holdouts of the arts of manuscript, Ghent and Bruges.

Bruges was not only the place where the medieval manuscript made its final stand; it was also where the English language found its way into print. It was in Bruges that William Caxton produced the first printed book in English, his *Recuyell of the Historye of Troye*, in 1473. Caxton is another remarkable example of the adventuresome souls drawn to the new technology of the press. A mercer, or dealer in luxury goods, he moved to Bruges in the 1450s, becoming the governor of the Company of Merchant Adventurers of London. Caxton made the translation from the French of the *Recuyell* himself, and in the more than one hundred books he produced he was famously, and influentially, devoted to his native tongue. But the urge was as much commercial as sentimental: with an already flourishing continental trade in Latin-language titles, Caxton—a canny merchant—knew he could break open a fertile new market in his own vernacular.

In the usage of Caxton's time, printing commonly was referred to as "artificial writing"—reminiscent of the way photography would later be understood and described as "drawing with light" when it first came into being. His influence on the course of English letters is unique, principally because he chose to publish so much in English so early, and because most of his books were translations of foreign works, which he accomplished as we say by his own hand, with his careful literalism rendering lengthy French sentences with careful fidelity. Caxton's own account of settling on orthography and vernacular in his translation work charts the simultaneous emergence of middlebrow taste and the market for printed books in English letters:

> Certainly it is hard to please every man, because of diversity and change of language. For in these days every man that is in any reputation in his country will utter his communication and matters in such matters & terms that few men shall understand them; and some honest and great clerks have been with me and desired me to write the most curious terms that I could find. And thus between plain rude and curious I stand abashed. But in my judgment the common terms that be daily used are lighter to be understood than the old and ancient English. And for as much as this present book is not for a rude uplandish man to labor therein, nor to read it, but only for a clerk and noble gentleman that feeleth and under-

standeth in feats of arms in love & in noble chivalry; therefore in a mean between both I have reduced & translated this
said book into our English not over rude nor curious but in
such terms as shall be understood by God's grace according
to my copy.

Caxton's influence on the world of English writing is unique—
both in its character and in the impact it exerted on the world
of letters that emerged as the English Renaissance. Caxton's
interests were broadly secular, narrative, and exotic; the catholic,
worldly sensibility that would fully burst forth with Shakespeare
is already a glimmer in his eye. A quick search of the Oxford
English Dictionary reveals Caxton cited as a source 22,543 times
in some 7,300 entries. For comparison's sake, Samuel Johnson's
Dictionary of the English Language is cited 1,413 times in 1,383
entries; Shakespeare is cited more than 60,000 times in 15,604
entries. The magnitude of Caxton's influence thus falls neatly
between that of the first great dictionary-maker and the most
renowned author in the language.

English was undergoing rapid change in the late fifteenth century. Caxton focused on the canonical poets of his day—but this
canon was a fleeting one, compelled to change in part by print; by
the early sixteenth century his successor, Wynken de Worde, was
printing the works of living poets, and the middle-English giants,
Chaucer and Gower, were rapidly waning.

The corrupting influence of writing on writing—the dangers
of copying from manuscript to manuscript—immediately arose
as a problem in the context of the printing press. It was articulated by Robert Braham, a very early editor in the world of the
English press, who in 1555 wrote about the importance of the editorial work undertaken when manuscript works were husbanded

into print. In an edition of the letters of John Lydgate's *Auncient Historie*, Braham talks about the editor's unweaving of the confusing warp of scribal transmission of a literary work, describing the editor of a volume of Chaucer as "a gentilman who laudably studyouse to yᵉ polishing of so great a Iewell, with ryghte good iudgement trauail, & great paynes causing the same to be perfected and stamped as it is nowe read, yᵉ sayde Chaucers workes had vtterly peryshed, or at yᵉ lest bin do depraued by corrupcion of copies, that at the laste, there shoulde no parte of hys meaning haue ben founde in any of them."

It's worth noting that the original sense of the word "pirate" with respect to literary work was used not to describe the unauthorized reproduction of someone else's work but the use of a printing press without proper license from the commercial or governmental authorities empowered to use and share the technology. It was not the work, but the means of production, that was the jealously guarded product. These powers were invested chiefly in royal governments, parliaments, and the printers' and booksellers' guilds, with the Church pursuing power of the press as well. In England a guild, the Stationers' Company, had been put in sole charge of the business of printing, a circumstance many found intolerable. The Stationers had been awarded the printing license by Parliament early in the seventeenth century as a matter of censorship and convenience. By depositing the power to print in the hands of the Stationers, the government explicitly sought to forestall the production of dissenting texts—and yet under the ostensible control of the book dealers, it could be argued that printing remained a commercial venture.

As with Gutenberg, Caxton and most of the English printers who followed him didn't hail from the scholarly or clerical estates. They were bourgeoisie, townsmen and merchants whose interests flowed through commercial channels. Theirs was a kind of cosmopolitan parochialism, at once fiercely tied to domestic ways and their native tongue and yet enriched by ideas—as well as revenues—that flowed across borders. With their guild affiliations, the first printer-publishers were pragmatic and programmatic; their lack of academic standing or clerical mandate made them both experimental (as with Gutenberg) and catholic in taste (as with Caxton). But it's also interesting that they were prepared to pursue lettered enterprise—to edit and collate, to process text; to translate, annotate, and compose. The broadly learned, inquisitive, enterprising distribution of learning—and a measure of intellectual courage to fuel it—seems to have appeared *before* the advent of the printing press that (so the classic argument goes) made it possible.

In the midst of all this capitalist spirit, the ethics of Protestantism thrived. It perhaps should not surprise us that an industry devoted to the powers of the written word would find itself so closely allied with a spiritual movement that placed the greatest possible value on scripture. Thus did Puritan works find their way into print, although many seditious printers lost their ears, their noses, and occasionally their lives. The secret English court of law known as the Star Chamber, in a 1606 case *de Libellis Famosis*, stipulated that truth was no defense against a charge of seditious libel—anything that would reduce public respect for the monarch or his officials was subject to punishment, regardless of its veracity. When one Puritan critic, Alexander Leighton, wrote and published a pamphlet in 1630 entitled *An Appeal to Parliament*, King Charles and his court were outraged. Leighton insisted that scripture was above everything, including kings; thus subjects could remain loyal while evaluating their rulers according to biblical standards. Leighton said his goal was to correct existing problems "for the honour of the king, the quiet of the people, and the peace of the church." The Star Chamber saw the situation differently, terming Leighton's work "seditious and scandalous." On November 16, 1630, Leighton was whipped at Westminster, and had one of his ears cut off, his nose slit, and one side of his face branded. One week later the mutilation was repeated on the other side.

The penalty did not stop other Puritans. John Bastwick, Henry Burton, and William Prynne were hauled into the Star Chamber in 1637 and charged with seditious libel for writing pamphlets that criticized royal actions. Each man was sentenced to "perpetual imprisonment" without access to writing materials, and the loss of their ears. The royal authorities, believing they had the populace on their side, proclaimed a public holiday highlighted by the public mutilations. But when the three men were allowed to make public statements (according to the custom of the day) as the officials waited with knives, they were cheered. Prynne was actually arrested and maimed twice; when he was released from prison and allowed to return to London, he was greeted by a crowd of 10,000 cheering supporters.

Barbarous attempts to control the press prompted even more determined opposition; as a *Boston Gazette* essayist would note more than a century later, the English Civil War had as its "original, true and real Cause" suppression of the press, and "had not Prynn lost his Ears, K. Charles would have never lost his Head." The verbal battle of Parliament versus Crown, Puritan versus Anglican, dissenters' grievance versus royal narrative, led to war during the 1640s. The changed political environment led to a journalistic surge of pamphlets, journals, and proto-newspapers, as Puritan-dominated Parliament, remembering past oppression, abolished in 1641 the torture-prone Star Chamber. The result, according to a parliamentary committee in 1643, was that many printers "have taken upon them to set up sundry private Printing Presses in corners, and to print, vend, publish and disperse Books, pamphlets and papers. . . ."

It was in the midst of the English Civil War, 1644, when John Milton—a frequent target of censorship himself—published the *Aeropagitica*, a pamphlet named for the hill in ancient Athens where orators had gone to contest the issues of the day. Milton argued that the suppression of the press cheapens society irredeemably. A free press, he held, allowed falsehood and error to find their way into daylight, where they could be exposed and killed; suppression of the means of reproducing writing damaged not only the false and the erroneous but the truth-teller as well:

> FOR BOOKS ARE NOT absolutely dead things, but do contain a potency of life in them to be as active as that soul was whose progeny they are; nay, they do preserve as in a vial the purest efficacy and extraction of that living intellect that bred them. I know they are as lively, and as vigorously productive, as those fabulous dragon's teeth; and being sown up and down, may chance to spring up armed men. And yet, on the other hand, unless wariness be used, as good almost kill a man as kill a good book. Who kills a man kills a reasonable creature, God's image; but he who destroys a good book, kills reason itself, kills the image of God, as it were in the eye. Many a man lives a burden to the earth; but a good book is the precious life-blood of a master spirit, embalmed and treasured up on purpose to a life beyond life. 'Tis true, no age can restore a life, whereof perhaps there is no great loss; and revolutions of ages do not oft recover the loss of a rejected truth, for the want of which whole nations fare the worse.

Milton's warning was well put. At the end of the century, John Locke complained that readers were "subjected to the power of these dull wretches who doe not so much as understand Latin"; in 1695 Parliament overturned the Press Act. Jealous of their monopolistic prerogatives, the Stationers lobbied Parliament assiduously for years to furnish some kind of protection for their right to print works for which they owned the license—arguing that such protections could be made beneficial to authors as well as printer-publishers. The remedy finally cobbled together, the Copyright Act of 1710 (often called the "Statute of Anne" after the queen in whose reign it was enacted) invested the license no longer in the means of production but the work itself. Although it seems second nature to a modern mind, this new view of the nature of literary production helped to renew Martial's ancient understanding of the word as a form of property. In the context of technologies of reproduction, this is an unstable, fuzzy formulation, the vexed and contradictory effects of which continue to pattern the cultural scene to this day.

Writing on the Wall

Of course, writing never is the property of any single class or interest; likewise, neither the page was ever the sole medium of letters. Inscription in stone is monumental, deeply permanent, and expensive; its ambitions are imperial and statist, yet also deeply personal; it is the graven letters of their tombstones, you'll recall, that give Pip in *Great Expectations* all his knowledge of his parents' ways and habits. But a wall needn't be incised to serve as a support for letters; plaster, wood, and masonry furnish not only shelter but ubiquitous, durable, and expressive media for the making and sharing of writing that was both public and ephemeral. Writing is an accompaniment to civilization, a form of life that takes place largely amidst walls: walls to shelter, walls to separate, walls to discipline and control. Graffiti is closely interwoven with the ways and rhythms of civil life, from ancient Roman cities like Pompeii to the megacities of today. And it hasn't always been illicit or criminal; the privative power of walls is not evenly distributed among civilized cultures.

Writing in more intimate forms—as letters, of course, but also in lockets and other treasured keepsakes—also has an effect on the form and power of the written word. Taking a look at George Puttenham's 1589 treatise *The Art of English Poesie*, historian Juliet Fleming detects in geometrical forms and layout of poetry, in the very disposition of words on the page, a lost literary aesthetic of embroidery, signage, and hornbooks. In the midst of the English Renaissance—the age of Shakespeare and the flowering of literature as a professional pursuit—literacy was broadly distributed, even while paper, pens, and printed materials were rare luxuries. And yet people were not mere passive readers; they inscribed their names and thoughts on every available surface. "Some people," Fleming suggests, "may have been able to sign their names in chalk but not with a pen."

This is a written world enlivened by diverse textures, by materialities beyond those of the page: letters carved in wood or punched and chased in silver, embroidered in tapestry and needlepoint, wrought in iron and worked into paintings, a world in which words are things—and in which, conversely, things also offer themselves up as words, as the figures of a divine and divinely scrambled message. This is writing that is contrived to take up space in the head *and* in the world of things, which in the early modern era were perhaps more coextensive realms than they are in the post-Cartesian world of today. As Fleming argues, for the English from the fifteenth to the early eighteenth centuries—the era historians call the early modern—writing's powers were "collective, aphoristic, and descriptive rather than individualistic, lyric, and voice-centered." Of course, there was nothing especially new about this in Renaissance England—remember the early use of the alphabet on Greek vases, the monumental inscriptions of ancient Rome, the carved stelae of classical China. Writing from the very start has never confined itself to purpose-made supports but has sought to infiltrate architecture and the landscape. "Graffiti" as a term first comes into use within the potter's craft, as *sgraffito*—an Italian word for carving clay to produce incised ware; it gains its modern specificity in the context of the archaeological discovery of inscriptions on the walls of Pompeii in the nineteenth century. In this usage graffiti had still not acquired the taint of the illicit, however; the Pompeiians' crude scribblings offered instead a flavor of revelation, retrospect garlanding them with the grandeur of the ancient and the rare.

We have the poet Allen Ginsberg to thank, however, for the modern sense of the word "graffiti." Ginsberg was a connoisseur and practitioner of writing on walls: the profane slogans he scrawled on the bathroom stalls nearly got him kicked out of Columbia University; later, in the New York State Psychiatric Institute on 168th Street (the Parnassus from which he would bring down *Howl*), Ginsberg noted the importance of wall-writing to inmates who were not permitted to converse with one another as normal human beings. It was Ginsberg who gave the name "graffiti" to such illicit, illegal, and offensive public scrawl—in explicit reference to the walls of ancient Pompeii, tying the angel-headed hipsters of the twentieth-century city to antiquity.

For Renaissance town-dwellers, however, graffiti had a more

practical mien. In a world in which memorization systems consisted of imagined palaces filled with mnemonic messages, the early modern mentality was structured as much by walls as by pages and leaves. The plastered walls of the early modern era made ready supports for writing in the home and in public; a simple application of whitewash readied the page for revision. Montaigne inscribed aphorisms on the rafters of his library. To Puttenham, an epigram is "but an inscription or writing made as it were upon a table, or in a window, or upon the wall or mantell of a chimney . . . where many merry heads meete, and scribble . . . with chalke, or with a cole such matters as they would every man should know, and descant upon." Queen Elizabeth I wrote a poem on a wall at Woodstock circa 1554, where it was seen and written down some forty years later:

> *Oh Fortune, thy wresting wavering state*
> *Hath fraught with cares my troubled wit,*
> *Whose witness this present prison late*
> *Could bear, where once was joy's loan quit.*
> *Thou causedst the guilty to be loosed*
> *From bands where innocents were inclosed,*
> *And caused the guiltless to be reserved,*
> *And freed those that death had well deserved.*
> *But all herein can be nothing wrought,*
> *So God send to my foes all they have thought.*

But wall writing could also be the reserve of the petty and the ill bred as well. George Herbert called a blank wall "the paper of a foole"; a stock character of Jacobean stage, Touchstone (best known from Shakespeare's *As You Like It*), appears in the scandalous comedy *Eastward Ho* (1605, by George Chapman, Ben

Jonson, and John Marston) as a small-minded shopkeeper who scribbles pious nostrums on his walls in lieu of gaining wisdom or learning:

> And, as for my rising by other men's fall, God shield me! Did I gain my wealth by ordinaries? no! by exchanging of gold? no! by keeping of gallants' company? no! I hired me a little shop, fought low, took small gain, kept no debt book, garnished my shop, for want of plate, with good wholesome thrifty sentences: as, "Touchstone, keep thy shop, and thy shop will keep thee;" "Light gains makes heavy purses;" "'Tis good to be merry and wise."

Writing leapt beyond the page from lovers' hands as well. The besotted wrote in candle smoke upon the ceilings of bedchambers, or wore "writing rings" set with a sharply cut diamond for incising words upon glass windows—a practice which survived into the nineteenth century, as when in the 1840s Nathaniel and Sophia Hawthorne, living in the Old Manse owned by their friend Ralph Waldo Emerson, etched newlywed sentiments into the windowpanes:

> *Man's accidents are God's purposes. Sophia A. Hawthorne*
>   *1843*
> *Nath Hawthorne This is his study*
> *The smallest twig leans clear against the sky*
> *Composed by my wife and written with her diamond*
> *Inscribed by my husband at sunset, April 3, 1843. In the*
>   *Gold light.*
> *SAH*

Emerson himself invoked the ancient, divine mandate of wall writing, modernizing Deuteronomy's mandates by announcing, "I would write on the lintels of the doorpost, *Whim*."

Today, we share a deeply felt modern sense of propriety with respect to writing's proper domains. Its seat is the printed page; even on the screen its role is secondary, merely informational, annotative. Writing that strives to take up public space requires the proper licenses and mandates: signage that is bought and paid for in the form of advertising or state-produced infrastructural writing that shapes the contours of street traffic and other modes of public movement. Even our persons are colonized by writing that is commercial and semiofficial in character, coming in the form of brands, team logos, and the surnames of professional athletes. Unmandated writing on public surfaces isn't even writing—it's graffiti, defacement, destruction of property. But writing is and always has been bigger than books, bigger than the page. Like the enclosure of the commons that drove rural people off the land and into the cities, turning peasants into wage earners, writing in the modern era was restricted by implacable degrees to the private page and the commercial space. The cover of a book is a kind of fence, a property line claimed by publishers, surveyed by editors, protected by the law. It's a turn we see in Touchstone's move above: by placing common nostrums within his own walls and claiming them as his own, Master Touchstone begins this transfer of a textual commons into private hands—long before copyright came along to provide the textual petit bourgeois with fence posts and barbed wire.

Perhaps Facebook got something right: for writing our selves, a wall is a better metaphor than a book; rather than fitting our electronic texts to the Procrustean bed of the book, we can look to walls, lockets, and doorposts, which find their digital analogues in blogs and feeds, mobile devices, and ever-present touchscreens.

Forms Most Wonderful

Although printers, writers, and readers worked unstintingly to sort out the effects and possibilities of the press, the technology of movable type changed very little for nearly four hundred years. The printing shop of Benjamin Franklin in eighteenth-century Philadelphia would have been entirely recognizable to William Caxton, Wynken de Worde, or Aldus Manutius; after a few minutes familiarizing themselves with new typefaces, they could have set down to work. But in the early nineteenth century, changes came to the technology of printing that would alter it fundamentally. The most important change came with steam power, automating the previously muscle-driven labor of printing. Soon, stereotyping emerged, allowing printers to prepare solid plates of type that could be used and reused in the printing of vast editions of copies. The output of the press increased a hundredfold, a thousandfold. Newspapers became cheaper and more widespread; printing appeared on a variety of media, including signs, handbills, cards, placards, shirt collars, fabric, boxes, and cans. The nineteenth century was the Age of the Letter, the soot-colored ink of the press seeping like coal fire into every corner of public and private life. In Europe and America, men even dressed like letters: their woolens dyed in inky tones, their top hats erect like the ascenders of the letters *b*, *d*, and *h*, their coattails and boot heels turned like serifs.

Even more than steam power, the invention of the telegraph

increased the ubiquity of letters in modern life. The uncanny warble of voices over a line, voices that are not quite voices, but utterance reduced to dots and dashes—

Faintly as from a star
Voices come o'er the line;
Voices of ghosts afar,
Not in this world of mine.
Lives in whose loom I grope;
Words in whose weft I hear
Eager the thrill of hope,
Awful the chill of fear.

The telegraph operator in Robert Service's poem suffers from an ironic loneliness—he's a node in a far-flung communication network, and his very connectivity is the cause of his physical solitude. He isn't entirely alone: working at a remote logging or mining camp, the telegraph operator serves as a bridge between his campmates and the outside world. It's to him the messages come across the Yukon's frozen taiga, singing of cities and warmth and bustle, wires humming with an uncanny, voicelike buzz—not actual human voices, of course, but letters in Morse code. Encoded by the telegraph operator, communications sped news from the hinterlands to the steam-driven presses of the city, strings of letters winging their way across continents and oceans to find their way into print. But for the telegraph operator, the effect of these voicings is distant and abstract, the speech of his comrades turned into machinelike bits and pieces, pulses of alien energy.

Despite its machinic nature, however, Morse code proved difficult for machines to parse—for like the lettering it encodes, it is irreducibly arbitrary. Telegraphy transformed the speed with which information could find its way into print, but it still required someone to copy out transmissions in real time and translate them into letters. In the late nineteenth century, various devices were contrived to render Morse code directly into printed characters; a decisive step was taken in 1876 by the French inventor Émile Baudot, who devised a code that represented characters by means of cyphers consisting of five binary units each. The units, which could be instantiated in the form of positive or negative electrical charges flowing over open telegraph wires, could encode as many as 36 (2^5) characters—plenty of amplitude for the twenty-six-letter alphabet, with room left over for combinations to encode spaces and punctuation; by specifying encodings for "character" and "figure," Baudot increased the capacity of his code to account for letters and numerals. Baudot's input device had five keys; operators input not the characters they wanted, but the code for each glyph. Multimedia by nature, Morse code can take the form of punctuated sound or blinking lights or flashing flags or puffs of smoke; even the human voice offers ready support for Morse. Like the voice, it's warm, arbitrary in its ups and downs.

Baudot, however, pointed the way to transmitting, decoding, and printing writing over telegraph wires. An Australian journalist named Donald Murray invented a machine to punch paper tapes with five-unit character encodings; the resulting tapes could be used to control typewriters or other printing machines to output printed matter automatically. Baudot and Murray's codes became International Telegraph Alphabets Nos. 1 and 2. And soon a host of new encoding emerged to specify linguistic variation—Cyrillic and Greek found their way into telegraphy, and the orthographic differences among Western languages found their way into unique flavors of telegraphic specificity as well. As telegraphy's international reach and significance grew in the late nineteenth century, government and industry groups in Europe and North America developed international standards committees to settle vexing disputes over the interoperability of various telegraphic systems. Baudot and Murray's systems gave birth to the teletype machine, which printed telegraph messages as they arrived, as strings of human-readable letters. Teletype terminals became ubiquitous in news organizations and businesses, and furnished the basis for Western Union's intensive network of telegram offices, which transformed personal communication in the middle of the twentieth century.

While the telegraph shot writing across continents and through undersea cables, the computational needs of rapidly growing nations increased. In the United States, the 1880 census took some eight years to tabulate; as the 1890 census loomed, it was clear that a new cycle of hand-tabulation would overtake the next decennial count. Statistician Herman Hollerith developed a system of machine tabulation using punch cards with which the census bureau managed to process the 1890 census in a single year. Punch cards were emphatically *not* writing; devised in the early nineteenth century to control the intricate weaves made by Jacquard looms, they were machine parts, specifying tasks for a given system to undertake in the correct order. Punch cards were modified to run other machines that required iterative modification of a narrow set of instructions—ins and outs; ups and downs—as well as player pianos and organs. In the mid-nineteenth century, Charles Babbage had recognized that punch cards could be used to record data as well, but Hollerith came up with a system in which electrical connections made through the punched holes could trip a mechanical adding machine, allowing his card system to record immense amounts of data on the fly.

Hollerith's company, the Tabulating Machine Company,

merged with three other firms in 1911 to become the International Business Machines Corporation, or IBM. Today we often think of computers as having emerged in the context of World War II and the postwar military-industrial complex—but the needs of a burgeoning, diverse population and a growing society were key to the development of crucial early components of computing technology.

And yet it would be a long time before we would learn to talk to machines, to exchange messages with them in something like recognizable human language using statements in written form. Hollerith's punch cards would remain the dominant means for putting information into computers, and for reading it out as well, into the 1960s; transforming those statements in and out of written, human-readable form required other steps and other machines. In the 1950s, a computer programmer rarely touched the machine that ran his programs; instead, he wrote out instructions, which an operator would translate into a deck of punch cards fed into the computer from a hopper. Not only were such computers architectural in scale, as is widely known; they also sat at the center of large computing bureaucracies requiring the tightly scheduled orchestration of workers performing a host of different roles.

The machines that were the forerunners of modern computers were built to embody the specific operations they were intended to perform; only later were the means found to reduce the instructions to a code that could be stored in some medium and played into the computer's switches to effect the desired operations. To program an early computer was to build it, to order and specify the relationships of its circuits and switches. These operations were purely mechanical, very far from writing in any recognizable definition of the term.

The frustrations and the ultimate ramifications of this approach

were apparent. The computer-science pioneer Alan Turing proposed a "universal machine" that could reduce diverse operations
to a code. "We do not need an infinity of different machines doing
different jobs," he wrote; "the engineering problem of producing
machines for various jobs [may be] replaced by the office work of
'programming' the universal machine to do these jobs." Turing
made this possible by taking apart the physical means of computation, reducing the puzzle-like logical operators to extensible code
that could be reconfigured to specify any computation.

By the 1960s, businesses and scientists were looking for more
convenient, less personnel-intensive systems for bringing computation into their work. In the early 1970s, a new class of machine,
the minicomputer, appeared. Compared to industrial workhorses
like the IBM 1401, such minicomputers as the Digital Equipment
Corporation's PDP-8 were underpowered, with an astonishing
8 to 16 bits of processing ability. But unlike the 1401, several of
them could be fit into a single room; priced around $20,000, they
were one or two orders of magnitude less costly than mainframe
computers. And crucially, they could be programmed directly, on
the fly, by a single operator working on the machine. And the system that was used to communicate with the computer's processor
and memory? It was the teletype machine—most frequently, Teletype Corporation's Model 33, which encoded characters using the
American Code for Information Exchange, a seven-bit character
encoding we know to this day as ASCII.

Descending from Baudot's code, the work of several generations
of international standards-making organizations, ASCII encodes
128 characters as poesies of 7 bits each, with an 8th bit added for
error-checking. A peculiar capacity of machine-based writing systems, the error-check bit adds a 0 or a 1 to the string of numerals. Mechanically, the electrical machinery of the telegraph can be

devised to "know" whether the sum of the numerals should be even or odd—and reject a message likely to be malformed or incomplete. In this respect most signally, Baudot's code differed from that of Morse: it was readable by both specially trained humans and specially devised machines.

Classically, the system offers ninety-five printable characters, including the majuscule (uppercase or "capital") and minuscule (lowercase or "little") letters and a close-knit tribe of punctuation marks and logograms like @, #, and the ancient "&" or ampersand—a scribal figure, a survival of the *et per se* with which medieval scribes ended the alphabet. Beyond these licit glyphs lie thirty-three "control characters," whose original purposes emerged from the technical needs of telegraphy: unseen glyphs whose job it is to tell teletype printers (now computers) to do various things with strings of characters. Control characters are digital shibboleths: the computer's version of the Turing Test, turned around to tell the digital machines from the fleshly ones.

Since the late 1980s, another character-encoding system, Unicode, has emerged to replace ASCII with a universal character set for computing. Unicode was developed to allow characters to combine and nest: to allow diacritical marks to stack on top of characters, for instance, or to combine the radicals of Chinese writing into the most complex characters. This is possible because Unicode, coded in 16-bit chunks rather than the 8-bit snippets of ASCII, can accommodate more than a million separate glyphs; to date, some 110,000 letters, characters, marks, and signs have been specified—more than 70,000 of them Chinese. The current set covered the vast majority of the writing systems in use around the world, along with a growing set of ancient alphabets, abjads, and syllabaries: cuneiform (specifically, classical Sumerian of the third century BCE), as well as Old Persian, Linear B, Egyptian hieroglyphs, and Byzantine musical notation, to name a few. It's safe to say that there is enough room in Unicode to exhaust all extant and abandoned writing systems, all the universal and ideal scripts, esoteric and angel-writing systems, fictional scripts like Klingon and Tolkien's Tengwar, and still leave enough scope for computers to invent scripts for their own amusement, should the fancy ever strike them.

Indeed, it's tempting to take the emergent, wholly digital discourses of writing to extremes, to imagine scenarios in which they escape our control. The great Polish science-fiction writer Stanisław Lem imagined a future literary field called "bitistics" devoted to the stories computers tell one another—narratives with their own abstruse poetics, a prosody of computation and cascading data, embodied in verse forms that have more in common with the structures of galaxies and living systems than sonnets or villanelles. In Lem's imagining, humans who study bitic literature will strive mightily to discern the existence of these ghostly computational epics—some of which the machines might compose to goad or trouble us, others of which they will inscribe only for themselves.

Stepping back from the speculative precipice of science fiction, however, we can find electronic writing invested with the same warmth, the same spectrum of human qualities, that enlivened the scribal roll, the medieval codex, and the modern novel. Recall the JavaScript snippet from the opening of the chapter: a written text that acts as a machine or a factory, or perhaps like a strand of DNA, unspooling its referents and resonances as endlessly reproducible collocations of symbols and effects. Such a script can produce any number of forms or surface texts: an audio player, an embedded video, a blog post, or a digital image of an ancient written text—

forms entangled with us, rich with our traces, our distinctly prolif-erative, tangled bank of expression.

Ghosts in the Machine

Looking back at the production of a large lectern Bible in Mainz we see our age shudder into being, with news, the republic of let-ters, and the corner bookshop all heaving aloft at the pull of his-tory's string like the sails of a ship in a bottle. In its own time, the transition between the written and the printed was not so sudden or discontinuous. The world changed, to be sure. But in crucial ways, within the compass of human life spans, much also stayed the same. Or perhaps it's more accurate to say that much that had taken expression in old forms found itself capable of new render-ings in new media. It was less a time of transformation, perhaps, then *translation*—a time that, in the midst of the shocks and trem-ors that seem to come with the rapid escalation of networked cul-ture, has much to teach us.

In his "Theses on the Philosophy of History," Walter Benjamin plays a series of variations on Paul Klee's 1920 painting *Angelus Novus*, imagining the figure as the angel of history: "Where we perceive a chain of events," Benjamin imagines, "he sees one sin-gle catastrophe which keeps piling wreckage upon wreckage and hurls it in front of his feet . . . a storm is blowing from Paradise; it has got caught in his wings with such violence that the angel can no longer close them. The storm irresistibly propels him into the future to which his back is turned, while the pile of debris before him grows skyward. This storm is what we call progress." It's an evocative image—and yet I think Benjamin has it turned around.

It is we who tend to see history as a single catastrophe rather than as interlocking chains of events.

The historian Adrian Johns argues that Gutenberg's invention wrought no single, easily identifiable revolution in the cultural history of writing. Instead it catalyzed a succession of diverse, local revolutions as authors and their various constituencies variously sought to do old things in new ways and to cloak novel things in familiar forms. Johns sees our transmodern world of networks and nodes, protocols and code, for all its vast differences from the age of Gutenberg and Caxton, as a similar mosaic of hopes and fears, of fanciful gambits and rearguard actions. "The implications of communications technologies will, of course, be wide-ranging and significant," concludes Johns, "but they are unlikely to be monolithic and hegemonic. They can best be understood and mastered with an appropriate knowledge of the cultural dynamics involved."

What a Tangled Bank We Weave

In *The Art of Memory*, her tremendous study of the role and meaning of esoteric memory techniques in Western scholarly culture, Frances Yates revisits the tale Socrates tells Phaedrus about the god Thoth's invention of writing, which the god-king Thamus disparages as "an elixir not of memory, but of reminding." As Yates points out, the story is often taken as an endorsement of pure orality, "a survival of the traditions of oral memory." But Yates argues that Socrates is talking not about memory in general, nor especially the art of mnemonics practiced by masters of memory. In Socrates's reckoning, she writes, the ancient Egyptians possessed memory of the deepest kind: memory of the Ideas—the living universal realities of which all things, passions, sensations, and sundry states of

affairs are but passing shadows. Memory in this view is no apparatus for the collation and curation of trivia but the imperishable
recollection of the knowledge we possessed before we are born—
the foundation of knowledge itself. "A Platonic memory," Yates
concludes, "would have to be organised, not in the trivial manner
of . . . mnemotechnics, but in relation to the realities." Memory in
the Platonic definition is not about storage but revelation.

Thus writing is thrown into an odd light: it becomes not the
great disrupter of the oral life world but a mere servant or species
of sophistry. The battle is not between the oral and the written
but between contemplation of the Ideas and the allure of false
wisdom. When one practices "artificial memory" by organizing
thoughts by arbitrary associations—the alphabet, or rhyme, or
superficial similarities of form and function—one is not recollect-
ing primordial Ideas that foundation reality; one is imprinting on
the brain those passing fancies and pretty pictures with which to
beguile and amuse. One is already writing. The actual making of
language-encoding marks is a mere idolatry of the Forms, setting
up zombielike letters in place of the imperishable Ideas.

Computer technology plays an Oz-like game: pay no attention
to the code behind the curtain. We don't really see what we read;
instead we see an instantiation, a ghostly apparition, an avatar. The
figures on the screen can only be read from one narrow angle; shift
one's perspective, and the illusion breaks into irresolvable shards.
Through hyperlinks, text invades and infects text; motion-capture
technology promises to make our very gestures into inscriptions.
Think of these ruptures, added to the shocks already delivered
by photography, film, and the broadcast media, and a conclusion
begins to suggest itself: the end of the regime not only of the alphabet, but of the self, in the parceling-out and networking of that
peculiar form of consciousness writing creates. Of course, writing

itself had *already* altered consciousness; the technologies that now emerge from it will alter that consciousness yet again, perhaps into forms unrecognizable to us from within writing's regime.

Recently, our attention has focused on this very splintering of attention, and the extent to which changing habits of hand and thought make different minds, different capacities, even (and especially) different imaginations. Does the supposed demise of handwriting presage diminishing educational outcomes? Can the success of Asian students in engineering and the sciences be attributed at least in part to the rigors of learning pictographic writing systems? These specific fears strike me as metonyms for larger, more amorphous anxieties—timorous responses to modernity, many of which precede the emergence of networked media and computers by a matter of centuries.

One of the most measured and searching explorers of these anxieties is the writer Nicholas Carr, whose 2011 book *The Shallows* plumbed the prospects of catastrophic cognitive, and hence cultural, change in the computer age. Carr's particular nexus of concerns arises in reflection on "neuroplasticity," an emergent understanding in brain science of the physiological changes taking place in the brain over the course of human development. Once considered a static organ, the mature human brain in recent years has been shown to be remarkably pliable and rewireable, and some of the most pronounced and best-studied changes in wiring take place in response to changes in the ways in which we feed the brain information. Of course, such rewirings transform our capacities, our sensitivities, even our sensibilities—and such change, Carr argued, might prove detrimental to our prospects.

In a chapter called "The Deepening Page," Carr offers a swift and graceful account of the history of writing. He traces the rise of logic, coherence, and depth from magical formulae scratched on

potsherds and wax tablets by the ancients through the pious allu-
sions of the Middle Ages to the graceful periodic sentences of the
eighteenth century. Their prose represented not only a formal triumph but a neural one as well. "To read a book was to practice an
unnatural process of thought," writes Carr, "one that demanded
sustained, unbroken attention to a single, static object." Such reading was valuable not just for the knowledge readers acquired from
the author's words but for the way those words set off intellectual
vibrations within their own minds. In the quiet spaces opened up
by the prolonged, undistracted reading of a book, people made
their own associations, drew their own inferences and analogies,
fostered their own ideas. They thought deeply as they read deeply.

To Carr, the story of manuscript, printing, and publishing is the
rise of the "deep page," with modern literature as the apotheosis
of literacy. The process that grimy old Gutenberg kick-started in
the fifteenth century culminates in Wallace Stevens, whose poem
"The House Was Quiet and the World Was Calm" glories in the
deep page: "The quiet was part of the meaning, part of the mind /
The access of perfection to the page."

The trouble is, it didn't feel this way to many people going
through these changes at various times in the past. Not to the
manuscript bookseller Vespasiano da Bisticci, who condemned
the coarsening presence of printed volumes in libraries devoted to
books in manuscript; not to Pope Paul IV, who started the Index
of Prohibited Books during the so-called incunable era following
the advent of movable type; not to Pope Urban VIII, who tangled
with Galileo; not to Jonathan Swift and Alexander Pope; not to
the French monarchy in advance of the Revolution. To many in
the midst of changes wrought, our minds and morals were changing too swiftly as they sought to stay afloat in the deepening page.

The printing press never *only* produced the kind of deep reading we admire and privilege today. It also produced propaganda and misinformation, "penny dreadfuls" and comic books offensive to public morality, pornography, self-help books, and much that was generally despised and rejected by polite culture. Readers in the eighteenth century in particular were offered a tantalizing selection of bawdy images and tawdry tales. As the great book historian Robert Darnton has shown, the age of Voltaire and Rousseau was awash in erotica, dirty cartoons, and fancifully libelous tales of the rich and famous. Any account of the history of "The Gutenberg Era" that lacks these is incomplete—just as any picture of our networked culture focused narrowly on LOLcats, SMS, and emoji is insufficient. We must consider both—for pornography, misinformation, and sheer foolishness have thrived from the age of incunables to the advent of the Internet. And the deep-reading brain changed, persisted, and evolved through it all.

The more traditional pundits and gurus who talk about the Internet often seem to want to draw strict boundaries between old mass-media culture and the more egalitarian forms taking shape online, between Internet life and life in the physical world. Sometimes the pointless-seeming jokes that spring from the Web seem to be calling a bluff and showing a truth: This is what egalitarian cultural production really looks like; this is what having unbounded spaces really entails; this is what anybody-can-be-famous means.

So where did the deep page come from? Not merely from ignoring the dross—for many alloys, and alliances, exist between poetry and pornography; at any given moment, it's never entirely clear which is which. Writing his "Battle of the Books" in 1704, Jonathan Swift depicted a war between canonical ancient and modern authors, with the ancients on the side of sweetness and light. But he didn't even trouble to critique the writers of bawdy, who were legion in his day; it was highbrow grandees like Descartes and classicist Richard Bentley who drew his ire more than any Grub Street hack. But the early modern reader of Swift's time engaged in an encounter not only with the luminescent wits of the Dial and the Royal Society but with a murky multiplicity of shifting possibilities in print: bawdy broadside cartoons, apocalyptic tracts, and libidinous mock epics from France. It was this multiplicity that produced the deep page—presumably, along with the brain circuitry underlying it.

Rather than fear the drying up of the deep page, we should marvel that it ever got deep in the first place—and we should remember as well that at the edges of the deep page lie miles of shallow estuaries: stinking, muddy—and teeming with life. Our plastic brains have been navigating their effluents for a very long time.

None of which is to say that changes in writing media don't change our brains. After all, what other explanation is there for the riotously diverse habits of mind, the manifold metaphors for making and learning and doing and growing, that writing in its many forms has given us? Shaving our quill with Occam's razor, we must admit that neuroplasticity is the physiological dimension of the changes in consciousness made by writing, which Walter J. Ong described in the middle of the twentieth century. After all, our technology, writing included, emerged from evolution—and for all its abundant variation, natural selection is quite conservative. Successful adaptations need stable foundations to persist in the face of all but catastrophic conditions. Humankind, curiously, has evolved to rely on its mutability for survival. Our intellectual flexibility—our cunning, tool-making, world-changing propensity—is itself adaptive (at least to date). And as such, it's built to survive. Perhaps the forms it takes—from cave paintings and music to hieroglyphics and the alphabet to cloud computing and motion-capture—are the various expressions of a single (albeit composite) trait. From search engines to barcode readers, the world of reading and writing isn't broken—it's expanding. Emergent technologies bear the traces of the life of writing; in a very real sense, they're its extension into new realms. To extend is in writing's nature—which is to say, it's in *our* nature. The rule of the alphabet is not tyrannical or dynastic; instead, it's another form or style, one among many that have arisen to teach us how to bring meaning forth out of the world's blooming, buzzing confusion.

Writing doesn't force or command; it teaches. The order it bestows on the emanations of human consciousness cultivates an architectural aspect to the imagination; into the forests and dark waters of myth and memory intrude the letters, those subtle conductors, cobbling together colleges and choruses of thought.

Many thinkers note that writing's ways seems to echo through cultural and social forms, offering not only tools but patterns by which to organize life. For thinkers like Ong, to whom the transition from oral to written culture loomed so large, this resonance is the force that shapes civilization, determining structures of governance, modes of narrative and argument, even consciousness itself. Does Western civilization really look like the alphabet? And if it does, is that because writing forces us into alphabetized boxes? Similarity doesn't imply causality—although perhaps it points to deeper causes. Writing didn't create our impulses to order, to compare, and to taxonomize; it built upon these inclinations and brought them to flower. That many cultural forms—from music to architecture to politics—participate in such flourishing doesn't point to an imperium of the alphabet but points instead to the more profound and rudimentary dispositions that evolved over millennia prior to writing's emergence. Different writing systems engage other evolved impulses. Ordered political structures, the column and the arch, patterns in weaving, music, and storytelling—they're like eyespots on the wings of butterflies, or orchids that evoke the sexual structures of insects. But we can take heart from this. For mimicry, symmetry, and economy aren't only the stuff of evolution but of poetry as well.

In this view, culture looks like a "reboot" of the riotous, implacable diversity that is such a prominent feature of life—a new platform, an open-source operating system compared to the massively parallel, simple-but-slow mainframe system that is biological evolution. Where biology provides a slow but certain nursery for the cultivation of adaptations, culture (ultimately a province of nature, albeit an infinitely capacious one) provides a kind of hothouse to nurture a rough-and-ready tool kit of means to survive. What culture seems to do is offer an adaptive circuit with a quicker feedback mechanism than raw natural selection, one that operates on a cycle much shorter than the reproductive cycles of a species. And writing, in this sense, is a signal development in the speeding-up and intensification of culture's capacity to develop new forms.

Reading of the kind held dear in the modern West was hardly birthed solely by the printing press; the exposure of medieval children to books and reading also paved the way. As Georges de la Tour dramatized in his painting *The Education of the Virgin*, books became an important component in domestic scenes: a candle, a glowing tome, and the rest of the world held in chiaracuroed abeyance. Such scenes of domestic bibliophily are by no means rare; as Nicholas Orme discusses in his great study *Medieval Children*, manuscripts provide repeated interpretations of this scene. *The Golden Legend* and the second-century apocryphal work the Book of James both report that Mary, daughter of the elderly and infertile Joachim and Anne, was sent to the Temple in Jerusalem for instruction. But artists persisted in imagining a domestic education for Mary, seated before her mother with an open book between them. These depictions often illustrate the first pages of Books of Hours, the medieval devotional books that began with the words of Psalm 51: "O Lord, open my lips, and my mouth will proclaim your praise. . . ." In this way, artists tied the intimate domesticity of shared reading with images of epiphany and oral surrender. Such scenes paved the way for books to engage the Western imagination in its deepest recesses, and help to bring the book down from its scholarly and liturgical heights to a matter of personal experience. To this day, books are domesticated for us by our childhood excursions among their pages—a critical period of reading that provides patterns for the book's place in civilization.

The warm and wondrous domesticity of early reading contrasts markedly with the ways in which children have historically learned to write. From cuneiform to the Palmer Method, the drills and sessions of rote memorization that accompany apprenticeship in the craft of writing have traditionally tended toward rigor, with occasional forays into outright abuse. With its complex nestings of language and graphic form, cuneiform must have been especially vexing and painful to learn. Students learned basic syllabic signs by rote in series running from the simplest to the most complex. Signs for the Sumerian syllables were but a small part of the system as a whole, however; the bewildering array of reconfigurations and juxtapositions that yielded a variety of alternate "pronunciations" came next in the curriculum, followed by lists of names and occupations, animals and objects. Finally, the copying of texts could begin—but in cuneiform, with its endless variations and punning alternatives, copying was also a form of composition. Scribal instruction was less like modern writing curricula than musical training, in which a performer practices the modes and keys and their attendant scales in order one day to play with well-tempered fluency. At the end of the process, the scribes of ancient Mesopotamia were profoundly skilled; their training included arithmetic and astrology, legal terminology and weights and measures. It was not so much a tuition in literary art but in cybernetics, the control of information—an ineluctable connection of writing with power that would influence not only the progress of society but literature as well.

But perhaps all this is changing as children increasingly acquire early writing skills not at school but at home. In the schools, literacy pedagogy comes and goes; at present the traditional phonetic, sound-based systems are resurgent, with so-called whole-language approaches taking a backseat. But while the classroom may change little (tablet computers and laptops notwithstanding), everything else about the reading environment has been transformed. Many children learn to use computers before their acquisition of literacy; and as computers become ever more embedded in the world of objects, so the transformation of reading becomes more intimate and profound. Perhaps technology disrupts the emergence of sustained reading, as Maryanne Wolf and other researchers worry. Or perhaps it helps to make the learning of writing happier, easier, more individually driven. Regardless, we'll get the readers we deserve, so to speak, who variously will transform and preserve the magisterium of writing in another cycle of culture's endless feedback loop. In days of old, we wanted scribes and scriveners who would take orders, and order our worlds thereby. Now we want flexible creators, makers of meaning; it's no surprise that the ways in which we learn to write change accordingly.

One of the most complex and highly evolved of all Darwin's endless forms, writing is evolving still to colonize new media and adapt to new modes of expression. Like chess, neoclassical architecture, and God, it is a thing that feeds on consciousness, requires it in order to survive and propagate. And yet to describe it thus takes away no grandeur or wonder from the magnificent contingency that is writing; indeed, it's the basis of my celebration. We're back on the tangled bank with Darwin, contemplating forms "so different from each other, and dependent upon each other in so complex a manner, [which] have all been produced by laws acting around us." Only in the case of writing, these laws act *through* us, not as dumb or blind agents but as the very work of our consciousness.

Writing is civilization's handmaiden and a tool of the powerful. It makes possible accounting, the law, and administered government. But in the space it opens up for literature, it has also ensured our freedom and vouchsafed our dignity. In similar fashion, we've seen computing as a technological revolution and a cultural cataclysm that fell upon us in the last half century like the angel of history crashing down from the clouds. But computers, like other machinic means of producing text from the printing press to the telegraph, are part of the history of writing, contiguous with the long phases in which manuscript was the only means of production. We've tended to think of networked culture as disruptive, a kind of "universal acid" dissolving worlds of writing and books and the learning they've nurtured over the past five thousand years. This disruption, however, is coextensive with and brought about not only by Gutenberg's invention but by flourishing discourses carried on in epistles and scriptures, inscriptions and graffiti scrawl—another chapter in the long story of the public sphere. We've tended to think of electronic writing as austerely disembodied, divorced from the warmth and materiality of "real" writing— its drying clay, plowed wax, stretched hide, and crisp paper. But its entanglements too are material, not only in the charismatic devices that body forth its signal but in the channels in which it flickeringly runs: copper wire and fiber optic, solder and silicon, and the farther ends of the electromagnetic spectrum.

Of course, even to pose dichotomies—a cycle of disputes between oral and literate, manuscript and print, the press and the computer—is to run into difficulties. For as we've seen, there never was only *one* kind of manuscript production, never a single medium in which handwriting could be produced. From the first, all four of the classical elements could make a medium for the written: skins and plant fibers, the stuff of parchment, papyrus, and paper, are all derived from living things, already amalgams of the elements; mineral inks marry earth and fire to water, all distilling a *logos* born in the breath and carried on the wind. And in electronic form, writing still mobilizes these material properties in expressive ways.

For the sake of writing, we raze forests and burn coal by the trainload—but these are mere scratches compared with the vast, Ozymandian ruin our other civilized habits threaten to make of the Earth. The crucial question is not whether our attention spans will evaporate, our cultural standards whither, our styles and genres fade. It is this: can writing help us undo what we have done with it? Whether in the form of spell or star gauge, scribal scrawl or machine-legible code, or in its increasingly abstruse and vibrant electronic modes, does writing give us the means to outpace, and ultimately to stay, the devastation wrought by our comprehensive material entanglements?

When the *Pioneer* space probes left Earth in 1972 and '73 on trajectories that would carry them out of the solar system, they carried plaques emblazoned with depictions of a nude Caucasian couple, various glyphs meant to help extraterrestrials identify the probe's astronomical origin and context, and a series of captions and messages encoded in a cipher based in binary mathematics. The astronomer and author Carl Sagan devised the plaque with Frank Drake, a pioneer of the SETI (search for extraterrestrial intelligence) research program; Sagan's wife, Linda Salzman, pro-

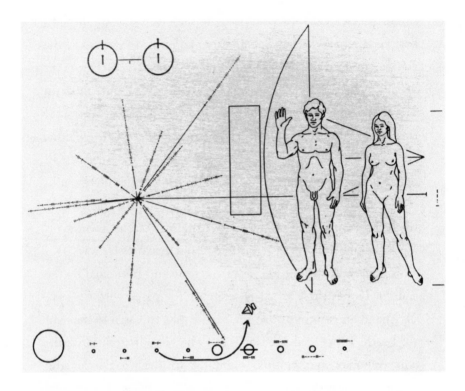

Meant as a timeless message to extraterrestrial intelligence, the Pioneer Plaque ineluctably speaks the scientific vernacular of its time, which mingled the promise of astronomical discovery with the fearful prospect of terrestrial annihilation. The glyph at the upper left is meant to represent an energy change in the hydrogen atom's single electron, to specify a wavelength used as a standard of measure in the mapping of our sun's position relative to a selection of other stars, conveyed in the starburst pattern running from left to right across the center. In the infinitesimal chance that one of the Pioneer probes is intercepted by an alien intelligence, there's no way to know whether Carl Sagan's carefully encoded message will disclose its information. But in its selection of scientistic measurements and human figures, its schematic depiction of the probe, and its fragile passage through the planets, the plaque expresses a semantic force and expressiveness that outstrip its syntactical ambition. I can't help but think of the Oxynrhynchus papyri, with their tissue of blocky Greek letters and wormy shreds and fibers knitting us together with our ancient ancestors, even as they underline the stretches of time that intervene.

vided the art. A few years later, Sagan recruited a team of experts in music, astrophysics, and recording technology to prepare the *Voyager* records, each of which was covered with a plaque based on the *Pioneer* model—as well as a tiny amount of purified uranium, incorporated into the electroplating of the record's cover, to act as an atomic timestamp, measuring the age of the probes on the scale of the 4.5-billion-year half-life of uranium-238.

No one can know whether aliens will ever decode Sagan's elegant, austere inscriptions. The odds against are, well, astronomical. As of this writing, the two *Voyager* probes are between 15 and 20 billion kilometers from Earth; transmissions, traveling over the Deep Space Network at the speed of light, take more than fifteen hours to bridge the gap. And yet despite the distance they've traveled, the probes are still in the solar neighborhood, mind-bogglingly far from other systems. *Voyager 1* won't pass within two light-years of another star system for some 40,000 years, and *Voyager 2* will come within five light-years of Sirius in about 300,000 years. The probes are now moving through the heliosheath, the outer layer of the sun's atmospheric influence, on the verge of interstellar space. Regardless of their speed relative to the Earth, in galactic terms they're very nearly stationary, joining the vast dance of stellar and dark matter in its stately, 250-million-year orbit of the Milky Way.

As Sagan himself admitted, the message of the probes was meant in the first instance for a contemporary, Earth-bound audience— to remind us that we're all in it together on the "tiny blue marble" of Earth—and secondarily to serve as a time capsule. In *Murmurs of Earth*, which documents the *Voyager* Golden Record project, Sagan tells the story of Esarhaddon, the seventh-century BCE Assyrian king who had inscribed plaques deposited in the foundations of monuments as messages for future times. Esarhaddon's monuments were carved from precious stone, bespeaking the meaning of beauty to the Assyrians and the power they found concentrated in it. Humans had long made sacrifices to send their wishes to the gods—votive offerings, from the Latin *votum*, or vow. A votive impulse consecrated not to the gods or to the dead but to the alien unknown or people of the far future, speaks to one of civilization's restless ambitions: the desire to be remembered.

There is even a probe with such a purpose, its plaque meant not for extraterrestrials but for the (equally alien) future inhabitants of Earth. The Laser Geodynamic Satellite, or LAGEOS, was launched in 1976 to facilitate the measurement of continental drift with a second LAGEOS set loose from the shuttle *Columbia* in 1992. The probe itself is a magnificent object, strikingly different from run-of-the-mill satellites: a ball of solid brass more than half a meter in diameter, weighing roughly 450 kilograms and dotted with reflectors like a large disco ball, LAGEOS carries no electronics or other instrumentation; it's a space-age artifact made with little more than Bronze Age technology. Essentially, it's a target: ground stations aim lasers at its reflective surface, measuring the distance to detect tiny perturbations in the Earth's crust. The probe's great mass helps it achieve a supremely stable orbit without on-board propulsion; it will be 8.4 million years before its orbit decays, at which time it will come crashing through whatever atmosphere remains in the wake of the epoch now called the Anthropocene. The LAGEOS plaque, also conceived by Sagan, features maps of the Earth's continents before and after the mission as well as at time of launch, spanning 16 million years of projected continental drift—permitting future Earthlings, human or nonhuman, to look at the disposition of the continents upon which they live and check our work.

There is a peculiar quality in these plaques and golden records—a compound of the Quixotic and the Ozymandian; an acknowledgment of our cosmic insignificance, paired with pride in the craft that pries that knowledge loose from the world—which is deeply characteristic of science in the late twentieth century. Sagan stated as much when he wrote of the first *Voyager* mission, "The launching of this 'bottle' into the cosmic 'ocean' says something very hopeful about life on this planet"—a hope that, however slim, was still vastly greater than the chance that one of the *Voyager*s would ever encounter life elsewhere. These messages in a bottle were among the more telling transmissions in a mythology of wonder that American science generated in the mid-twentieth century— an attempt, through science itself, to preserve a record of life on Earth, in light of destructive powers unleashed by science in the atomic age.

Some have tried, through writing, to warn future Earthlings of the destructive powers that our civilization has unleashed. In the early 1990s the US Department of Energy commissioned a panel, which included artists, technologists, and scientists (including Frank Drake and Jon Lomberg, Carl Sagan's collaborators), to devise a warning message future discoverers of our nuclear-waste storage sites. In 1993 the so-called Marker Committee presented their report, in which the authors addressed the challenge of communicating with interlocutors more than 10,000 years in the future—a time span twice the length of writing's history to date. They proposed that various design elements be introduced in the landscape, including fields of foreboding spikes and black obtruding stones. But inescapably they fell back on writing:

This place is a burial place for radioactive wastes. We believe this place is not dangerous IF IT IS LEFT ALONE! We are going to tell you what lies underground, why you should not disturb this place, and what may happen if you do. By giving you this information, we want you to protect yourselves and future generations from the dangers of this waste.

They imagined this legend, this bleak spell from the age of science, to be engraved in stone on the walls of a kind of shrine hidden in the earth—to be discovered at the entrance to the disposal site, yet not deep enough that readers would be exposed to the silent, invisible ravages of the waste.

> Radioactivity declines exponentially with time. By 10,000 years after the waste was buried here, the waste will be no more hazardous than the ore from which the radioactive material was taken. . . . There is a picture showing the four brightest stars that can be seen from the site (Sirius, Canopus, Arcturus, and Vega). The position of the star-rise changes in time, and lining up the angles of the star-rise with the map will show how much time has passed since the site was closed.

Here, the committee's warning turns a note of the scientific sublime, indicating our discovery of the gorgeous enormity and cold longevity of the cosmos, which accompanied our revelations of the nature of matter and energy. And they conclude with an admonition to rely on writing's ancient rituals, delivered in the simple prose of modernity:

> Do not destroy these markers. If the message is difficult to read, rewrite the message in your language in the blank area on this wall. If the markers are worn or missing, add new ones in longer-lasting materials in languages that you speak. This

site, built in . . . by the United States of America government, represents a first attempt to responsibly dispose of wastes for an extended period of time.

Look on our works, ye mighty, and despair.

The message has not yet been inscribed, much less delivered. Politically and culturally, we have not yet come to grips with the enormity of our long-term impact on the planet, the catalogue of which extends beyond radioactive waste to encompass habitat destruction and mass extinction, pollution, and climate change. In North America, the construction of adequate facilities for the long-term storage of radioactive waste has proven politically impossible, and the sites that exist here and elsewhere around the world are far from ready to close and seal off. Thus the extant messages our civilization has left for the *longue durée* remain hopeful, triumphant. Plaques on the *Apollo* landers, now lodged on the moon, read, "We came in peace for all mankind"; but the Marker Committee's message—which as yet has not been emblazoned on plaque or stone—may be the truest and most urgent message our civilization could offer to future generations.

What will survive, of course, won't be these celebratory apostrophes and dire warnings—in any case, not ever as they were intended. It will be the many-colored, provisional jumble of writing in toto, fragmented and scrawled, that our descendants will be left to decipher: the clay shards and well-rubbed papyri, the clumsy-looping window scratches and elegantly indecipherable graffiti. A palimpsest of palimpsests, letters overlying letters, both shoving one another down and urging one another on. Writing arose as an instrument of already-complex human societies, the endowments and outputs of which now threaten not only our species but the very future of life itself. It's far from clear that writing will help us to avoid the destructive forces civilization has unleashed. But one thing we can depend upon: for its ubiquity and durability, its proliferative vitality, its urge to record and connect and knit itself into the warp of the world, our writing will outlast ourselves.

PAGE AS MIND

"What else than a natural and mighty palimpsest is the human brain?" I write out De Quincey's question, with which this book began, a second time. How has it changed in light of the 60,000-some words that intervene?

Thomas De Quincey was a Romantic, in touch with both the animal basis of human ingenuity and its highest, most exalted forms. We call him a Romantic largely because at the age of fifteen he read the *Lyrical Ballads* and broke out of his dreary boarding school to go find William Wordsworth. On that attempt he made it as far as his mother's house—although eventually he would spend a good deal of time with Wordsworth, living in the poet's former abode, Dove Cottage in the Lake District, turning to writing whenever he was short on cash—a recourse one hears of rarely nowadays—and taking a good deal of opium when he wasn't.

From his opium visions, De Quincey crafted two collections of rambling, spinning, mad essays called *Confessions of an Opium Eater* and *Suspiria de Profundis*, the latter of which is often translated as "sighs from the depths" but might more simply be called "deep sighs." It was in *Deep Sighs* that he wrote about the palimpsest. Before this time, a palimpsest had been understood straightforwardly as a piece of used parchment or vellum scraped clean, erased as it were, for a writer's reuse. Even in De Quincey's early nineteenth century, paper remained expensive; writers of letters would often fill a page and then turn it ninety degrees and fill it again, thus palimpsesting—for it could be used as a verb—themselves. When scholars became interested in the antique, the palimpsest would prove a crucial source in philology for the reconstruction and recovery of lost texts, a role that palimpsests still serve today in rare-books libraries and archives. But De Quincey noticed something else about the palimpsest: that it offers a handy metaphor for the workings of the human brain.

De Quincey begins with the material facts of the palimpsest, focusing peculiarly on its economics: its role as an index of the brute, material dimension of shifting tastes and cultural change. As an author's cultural stock declines in value, the material on which her work was expressed (although, with De Quincey, the pronoun is always masculine) becomes an object of desire. "Once it had been the impress of a human mind which stamped its value upon the vellum," he observes; "the vellum, though costly, had contributed but a secondary element of value to the total result. At length, however, this relation between the vehicle and its freight has gradually been undermined. The vellum, from having been the setting of the jewel, has risen at length to be the jewel itself; and the burden of thought, from having given the chief value to the vellum, has now become the chief obstacle to its value; nay, has totally extinguished its value, unless it can be dissociated from the connexion." Thanks to these merely fortuitous economics, De Quincey observes, successive generations left us records of the past—and with this record, an irony: for it was precisely each intervening generation's desire to overwrite, to efface—*to forget*—that made the preservation possible. "They did the thing proposed to them: they did it effectually; for they founded upon it all that was wanted: and yet ineffectually, since we unravelled their work; effacing all above which they had superscribed; restoring all below which they had effaced." Whether through impatience or hostility, De Quincey is saying, writers erase and overwrite their predecessors' words—and by so doing, in the form of the palimpsest, they preserve the traces of those past words and add to their preciousness and significance. "Such a palimpsest is my brain; such a palimpsest, O reader! is yours. Everlasting layers of ideas, images, feelings, have fallen upon your brain softly as light. Each succession has seemed to bury all that went before. And yet in reality not one has been extinguished." De Quincey notes that "the vellum palimpsest, lying amongst the other *diplomata* of human archives or libraries," often contains layers that are strangely and even comically conjoined, an enjambment that is "fantastic or which moves to laughter, as oftentimes there is in the grotesque collisions of those successive themes, having no natural connexion, which by pure accident have consecutively occupied the roll. . . ." Yet with the mental palimpsest comes a difference: for while the layers of text written and overwritten on vellum by successive generations are linked only fortuitously, the mind always strives to make connections: "in our own heaven-created palimpsest, the deep memorial palimpsest of the brain, there are not and cannot be such incoherencies."

Making meaning out of the merely fortuitous: it's what the written word needs of us, has called us to aid it in, all these millennia. Such was apparent to Ezra Pound, whose fascination for the immediacy and imagistic force of the Chinese letter was matched by an awe for the culture that could be made with machines. For all his contempt for Victorian decadence in verse, Pound appreciated the industry and inventiveness of the era in which he was born. As critic Hugh Kenner has shown, those inventions—the typewriter in particular—offered Pound and his confreres more than mere tools, but a whole ars poetica of invention. The modern machine, and industry itself, might have seemed to Pound like a mighty palimpsest, resting upon the inventions of past generations, linking them together in systems with meanings sometimes convenient, often terrible, but unambiguously sublime. And this machinery, for a modern poet like Pound, articulated with the world of word-making as well. "Like high-tension steel," Kenner observes, Pound recognized that "a rhythm can be an invention."

"Poems are made of words," Kenner continues, "but more than words. They are made of all the devices by which the words, and the way we hear them or see them, can imply melody, and gesture, and intonation, even facial expression."

The implications of gesture, intonation, facial expression: these too find their way into the written word. Cramped hands, tired eyes, and addled brains are the occupational hazards of the scribe, frequently bemoaned in medieval marginalia—but more than this, they are also objective correlatives for the ennui, envy, and anxiety that stalk the writer through history. Even when produced by the algorithmic machinations of computers, the written word is a thing made by organisms—and a thing that remakes those organisms in turn. In the Enlightenment, the organism was likened to a machine, an ordered arrangement of articulated parts; the human organism, moreover, was a machine with a governor, a homunculoid ghost in the works, pulling the levers with serene rationality. Romantics like De Quincey rejected this model. For them, the organism was a haunted thing that haunts the world, less a machine than a storm of desires, sensations, forces, and effects—a palimpsest of meat and meaning, with all its layers in communion. Even machines aren't machines in the way we like to think—for they too are linked to one another through time. They depend upon one another, and ultimately on us, to give them the motive force of meaning.

Still, the Enlightenment's little governor never went entirely away. In our own time it persists, distributed throughout the network, no longer seated at the controls but content to act as a property, hidden in the etymology of the *cyber*—which, after all, is derived from the ancient Greek word for "governor." Ultimately, however, the cyber is us: people pushing things around—symbols, chisels, quills, press forms, keys, regions of electrostatic charge. As we talk about the digital, we acknowledge that numeracy, too, is a species of the written word, that counting is a thing done upon the fingers, a thing which, although it reaches into the ideal and the abstract, begins with earthly substances made into symbols. However finely fibered, however far its reach, my computer still does the work of my own hand. And that work, however much it may seem beyond my ken, is my responsibility to shape and shepherd.

In this shepherding, I circle back once more to the question of De Quincey's question, posed once at the start of this book and again here at the close—and posed moreover in writing, the peculiar effects and resonances of which I hope seem apparent by now. For in fact I copied the words using the keystroke "command-c," and then "pasted" them, complete with supporting punctuation, typeface, and font stylings, from the top of the document in which I'm composing the book.

How does this act differ from the uncanny copying of Freud's Magic Writing Pad, with the ghosts of scribbled letters plowed into the wax? How different is it from the blottings and erasures of Martial or Saint Paul? I copied the first instance of De Quincey's question by transcribing the passage from a reading of an electronic text in a format that doesn't support copy/paste, forcing me to key in the words. Those key-taps—registered as events by the committee comprising the computer, the network, and the code that runs the web-based word processor I use—were archived in an unseen data table so that I can retrieve and make use of them later.

Ten years after beginning this book in earnest, it has spread bits of itself across many such tables, in information packets flung about the world from server to server, and in the bones of files in numerous versions of three or four text-editing programs. And in this uncanny phenomenology of writing in the twenty-first century, the palimpsest I've made of De Quincey's question turns its terms around: from the metaphor of the mind as a page to the seeming possibility that the page—the very one upon which these letters are appearing to me in the 12-point font of the Georgia typeface—is a kind of mind as well.

Martial's sponge lifted a limpid trace of damp ink from the striated surface of the papyrus; in medieval hands, the penknife flaked and chipped at a sheen of iron-gall ink until enough vellum fiber had given way to ghost the letters into near oblivion. To recopy a passage as I have done here, scribes in times past turned variously to memory, oral discourse, and to tumbly, dingy bits of movable type. Now, bits of messages fling about over circuits, whirling together in command performances of letters, words, and passages new and old. Is this new kind of page a mind—a mind to overturn the mind-as-page? I don't think the outcome is so simple. For across all of these surfaces, it is human relationships—among us all as readers, thinkers, and writers—that set the temper of the music we make. Those relationships eventuate in code now, in software, as much as the hierarchies of the schools, the tutelage of calligrapher and pupil, or the terse contract of writers and publishers. And it's through our relationships that we make minds of people and pages, all of us together in the written word.

ACKNOWLEDGMENTS

This book emerged through a time of tremendous change in the worlds of writing and worlds of my own, and I owe a great debt of gratitude to my editor at Norton, Alane Salierno Mason, for her sagacity, consideration, and patience above all.

Early work on *Palimpsest* took shape just as the social media came into bloom, and I carried on a wide-ranging seminar with many friends and colleagues through its flickering agency. Crucial examples and key concepts formed and were put into play via blog post and Tweet, sustained and fueled by conversation with friends and colleagues—some of whom I have yet to meet in person—including Elise Blackwell, Tim Carmody, Alan Jacobs, Matthew Kirschenbaum, Tim Maly, Joanne McNeil, Robin Sloan, and Anne Trubek, as well as a host of friends, followers, and fellow travelers too numerous to name. In toto they fortified me and the work (the many faults of which I retain enough individuality to claim as mine alone).

Since 2011, I've been fortunate to be appointed with metaLAB, an experimental teaching and research unit at Harvard, head-quartered at the Berkman Center for Internet and Society. Both the Center and the lab are remarkable cauldrons of intellect and impact; I'm especially grateful to have been included in the Berkman community, which sustains many of us through its brew of collegiality, camaraderie, and inspiration. I've relied on the intellectual and creative energy of all my metaLAB colleagues, some of whom—in particular, Yanni Loukissas, Cris Magliozzi, Kyle Parry, and Jeffrey Schnapp—offered critical insight as the book neared completion. And I must offer thanks as well to an anonymous, helpful cohort, a band of happy centurions, an army of heady correspondents. They know who they are.

I'm grateful to a number of magazine editors with whom I've worked through these fraught years for the republic of letters—especially Joshua Benton of the *Nieman Journalism Lab*; Alexis Madrigal, *The Atlantic* Technology Channel; and James Mustich and Bill Tipper of the *Barnes and Noble Review*. Some passages of this book first appeared in articles for the *Boston Globe* ("Ancient Evenings," a review of *The Buried Book* by David Damrosch, March 4, 2007) and the remarkable *Aeon Magazine* ("The Ache for Immortality," February 19. 2013).

I close this book in memory of two remarkable persons. First, Aaron Swartz (1986–2012), whose commitment to writing's electric, emancipatory magisterium made the Internet more visible, liberating, and beautiful. Secondly, I want to invoke my sister-in-law, Judith Schlesinger (1967–2008), who died while this book was midway on its journey. D. H. Lawrence wrote that the departed rustle like migrant swallows in the roof-eaves of our minds; for me and my family, some of these birds of passage take form as the journals where Judith, from the very first she could write, formed a record of her budding genius and generosity of spirit. Now they make a toppling stack of composition books, pages ruffled by years of ballpoint making the slow transition from block letter to cursive to quick adult hand. They could never render her in full, much less replace her. But for her sisters, her husband, and her children, they do offer a provisional and sustaining intimacy, a life in longhand— final and most cherished proof of the undying power and teaching that writing is given, and gives.

Notes on Sources

Books in Running Brooks

Emily Dickinson wrote "A letter is a Joy of Earth" in a letter to Charles H. Clark now kept at Amherst College, where it is Amherst Manuscript #776, page 2. It was published first in the *Letters* (1894), and subsequently as verse; it appears as #1672 in the Franklin *Variorum*. I quote Isaiah 4:16 from the New International Version of the Bible. Lacan's words ("A letter always arrives at its destination") appear in his "Seminar on the Purloined Letter," which may be read online at http://www.lacan.com/purloined.htm; they appear at the very end; it also may be found in *Ecrits: The First Complete Edition in English*, translated by Bruce Fink (W. W. Norton, 2007). The story it concerns is one of Poe's most ingenious.

Duke Senior's line ("tongues in trees") occurs in *As You Like It*, Act II, Scene 1, in the speech that begins the scene. Darwin's line about the "tangled bank" occurs in the concluding paragraph of *On the Origin of Species*, and appeared in the first edition of the book, published in 1859 by John Murray; I accessed the Project Gutenberg plain-text version of the first edition of *Origin* (http://www.gutenberg.org/files/1228/1228.txt). Sigmund Freud's "A Note Upon the Mystic Writing Pad" first appeared in English in *General Psychological The-*

ory (1925), as Chapter XIII. John Stuart Mill's remark on "character" may be found on page 112 of *On Liberty* in the edition published by Walter Scott Publishing in 1901; there is a Project Gutenberg version of this text, which I accessed in HTML (http://www.gutenberg.org/files/34901/34901-h/34901-h.htm). Richard Sennett's *The Craftsman* was published by Yale University Press in 2008; I quote from page 184. Stephen Jay Gould elaborated his idea of "non-overlapping magisteria" in a 1997 essay for *Natural History* magazine, later reprinted in the volume *Rocks of Ages: Science and Religion in the Fullness of Life* (Ballantine, 1999); he can't be blamed for my use of the term.

ORIGINS AND NATURE

Eric Gill asserts that "letters are things" on page 120 of his *Autobiography*, published by Biblo & Tannen Publishers in 1968. *Kalevala* selections come from John Martin Crawford's nineteenth-century translation of the Finnish national epic wrestled to life by Elias Lönnrot (*Kalevala: The Epic Poem of Finland*), an edition of which is available via Project Gutenberg (http://www.gutenberg.org/cache/epub/5186/pg5186.html). The passages describing Odin's torments hanging from the world-tree Yggdrasil are excerpted from *The Elder Edda of Saemund Sigfusson*, translated by T. H. Smart, privately printed in 1905.

John Dee documents his angelic conversations—and lays out his "Enochian Alphabet"—in *True and faithful relation of what passed for many yeers between Dr. John Dee . . . and some spirits* (and that's the short-title version!), printed in London by D. Maxwell for T. Garthwait, 1659. Of Socrates and his critique of writing, it's worth recalling that the story comes to us through the agency of Plato, who is richly resident in writing's magisterium. The tale of Thoth, and the critique of writing, occur in the *Phaedrus*, which is translated and reprinted in the many editions of the *Dialogues*; online, the indispensable authority for all things classical is the Perseus Project, where *Phaedrus* may be found (http://www.perseus.tufts.edu/hopper/text?doc=Perseus%3Atext %3A1999.01.0174%3Atext%3DPhaedrus). The version here is adapted from Benjamin Jowett's citation of the *Dialogues* first published between 1871 and 1875 by Oxford's Clarendon Press. The story of Kalamos and Thoth is my notion and has no mythic antecedent of which I'm aware.

Claude Lévi-Strauss elaborates his concept of "bricolage" in *The Savage Mind*, which I have in the 1966 edition, published by the University of Chicago Press (originally published, in French, as *Le pensée sauvage*, published by Librarie Plon in 1962). Stanislas Dehaene recounts the work of his lab on the neurophysiology of reading in *Reading in the Brain: The New Science of How We Read* (Penguin Books, 2010). R. Dale Guthrie conjectures on the nature of the art of the Pleistocene in *The Nature of Paleolithic Art* (University of Chicago, 2006). "Neoteny" is a basic concept in developmental biology, which I first learned about in Stephen Jay Gould's *The Mismeasure of Man* (W. W. Norton and Company, 1996). The transmission of the Ammassalik wooden map is documented on pages 246–50 of the *Danish Konebaads-expedition to Greenland's East Coast*, Gustav Holm's 1885 account, in Danish, of his eastern Greenland journey. The just-so story of the handy, buoyant wooden map is told in Bill Buxton's *Sketching User Experiences: Getting the Design Right and the Right Design* (pages 36–37), published by Morgan Kaufmann in 2007.

PICTURES AND THINGS

I took an introductory course in Mandarin, taught by my friendly and wise Harvard Library colleague Ray Lum; much of my understanding of the workings of *hanzi* comes from that experience (and no mistake or confusion on my part is Ray's responsibility, or anyone's but my own). The documentation of the origins of Chinese writing is vast;

see Florian Coulmas, *Writing Systems of the World* (Blackwell, 1991); William G. Boltz, *The Origin and Early Development of the Chinese Writing System* (American Oriental Society, 1994); David N. Keightley, *Sources of Shang History: The Oracle-Bone Inscriptions of Bronze-Age China* (University of California, 1978); and David N. Keightley, "Art, Ancestors, and the Origins of Writing in China," *Representations* 56 (1996), 68–95. John DeFrancis's *Visible Speech: The Diverse Oneness of Writing Systems* (University of Hawaii, 1989), a polemical work arguing for the Romanization of Chinese, includes an account of the history and a critique of ideas of the "objectivity" and "universality" of ideograms. Ha Jin's story appears in the collection *Ocean of Words: Army Stories* (Vintage, 1998). The story of Mao's simplification campaign is the focus of Richard Kraus in *Brushes with Power: Modern Politics and the Chinese Arts of Calligraphy* (University of California, 1991). The *Chinese Recorder and Missionary Journal* was published in 1871 in Foochow (Fuzhou); the copy I consulted, held by Harvard College Library, was digitized by the Google Books Project (http://books .google.com/books?vid=HARVARD:32044079398210&print-sec=titlepage#v=onepage&q&f=false). It is discussed, along with Emerson's approach to Chinese writing and thought, in Donald Murray, "Emerson's 'Language as Fossil Poetry': An Analogy from Chinese," *New England Quarterly* 29, no. 2 (June 1956), 204–15. Joshua Marshman's work is *Elements of Chinese Grammar: With a Preliminary Dissertation on the Characters, and the Colloquial Medium of the Chinese, and an Appendix Containing the Ta-Hyoh of Confucius with a Translation*, printed by the Mission Press at Secampore (Singapore), 1814. John Francis Davis's *Poeseos Sinicae commentarii: The poetry of the Chinese* was published by Asher in London in 1870. I consulted the *Journals* of Ralph Waldo Emerson in the edition made by Edward Waldo Emerson and Waldo Emerson Forbes published in 1909 by Houghton Mifflin's Riverside Press and digitized by the Internet

Archive (https://archive.org/details/journalsofralphw02emeruoft). Emerson's comments on Thoreau I first came across in Robert D. Richardson's *Emerson: Mind on Fire* (University of California, 1996). The transcendentalists' takes on Chinese writing and thought, and their relationship with Sung-dynasty scholarship, are discussed by Hongbo Tan in "Confucius at Walden Pond: Thoreau's Unpublished Confucian Translations," *Studies in the American Renaissance* (1993): 275–303. Ezra Pound's "In a Station of the Metro" appeared in the April 1913 edition of *Poetry*, and can be consulted on the magazine's website (http://www.poetryfoundation.org/poetrymagazine/poem/1878). My understanding of Pound and Fenollosa's work depends crucially on *The Chinese Written Character as a Medium for Poetry: A Critical Edition*, edited by Haun Saussy, Jonathan Stalling, and Lucas Klein, published by Fordham University in 2008. Fenollosa's essay "The Coming Union of East and West" appeared in the *Harper's New Monthly Magazine* 98, no. 583 (page 115). My source for the connection of writing to Chinese health philosophy is John Hay, "The Human Body as a Microcosmic Source of Macrocosmic Values in Calligraphy," in *Theories of the Arts in China*, Susan Bush and Christian Murck, eds. (Princeton, 1983), 74–102. David Hinton's translation of the *Analects of Confucius* (Counterpoint, 1998) is a terrific source. The topology of writing systems is discussed in M. Changizi, Ye H. Zhang Q, and S. Shimojo, "The Structures of Letters and Symbols Throughout Human History Are Selected to Match Those Found in Objects in Natural Scenes," *American Naturalist* 167, no. 5 (May 2006), E117–39. For my account of Su Hui's "Armillary Sphere" I depend upon David Hinton's discussion in *Classical Chinese Poetry* (Farrar, Straus & Giroux, 2010), 105–9; Hinton's own version of the poem is online at http://www.davidhinton.net/#!classical-chinese-poetry-an-an/ckk5. Xu Bing's work *The Book of the Sky* is documented in *The Art of Xu Bing* (Britta Erickson, Sackler Gallery).

WRITING AND POWER

Walt Whitman's "Calamus" is collected in *Leaves of Grass*; my source is the Library of America edition *Walt Whitman: Poetry and Prose*, published in 1982. I use the edition of Claude Lévi-Strauss's *Tristes tropiques* translated by John Weightman, published by Penguin in 1992. I read Jean-Jacques Rousseau's "Essay on the Origin of Languages" in *On the Origin of Language: Two Essays* (Rousseau and Johann Gottfried Herder), translated by John H. Moran and Alexander Gode (University of Chicago, 1986). Rousseau's "Social Contract" I find in the edition of *The Basic Political Writings*, translated by Donald A. Cress and published in 1987 by Hackett. Robert Graves's notions about the runic alphabet are elaborated in *The White Goddess: A Historical Grammar of Poetic Myth*, first published by Farrar, Straus & Giroux in 1948. David Damrosch recounts the impact of Gilgamesh in *The Buried Book: The Loss and Rediscovery of the Great Epic of Gilgamesh* (Holt, 2007). Max Weinreich's observation on the precariousness of the "dialect" comes from a 1945 speech, published in *YIVO Bleter* 25:1. Henri Michaux's words on Chinese writing come from his *Ideograms in China*, translated by Gustaf Sobin and published by New Directions in 2002. John Man's account of the origins of Greek writing appears in *Alpha Beta: How 26 Letters Shaped the Western World* (Wiley, 2001). I go back to the Perseus Project for Hesiod's *Works and Days* (http://www.perseus.tufts.edu/hopper/text?doc=Perseus%3Atext%3A1999.01.0132%3Acard%3D1). E. R. Dodds's text is *The Greeks and the Irrational* (University of California, 1951). Eric A. Havelock's arguments about writing and ancient Greek culture are most famously set forth in *Preface to Plato* (Harvard's Belknap imprint, 1982) and *The Muse Learns to Write* (Yale, 1988). For the Carolingian scribal tradition, see *Alcuin: His Life and Legacy* by Douglas Dales, published by James Clarke & Co., 2012. Falconer

Madan recounts scribal practices in *Books in Manuscript: A Short Introduction to Their Study and Use*, published by Trench, Trübner & Co. in 1893. Charles Dickens tells Pip's story in *Great Expectations*; I have the Norton Critical Edition published in 1999, and I've quoted from chapters 9, 49, 53, and 57. Hamlet discusses erasure from the tables of memory in Act I, Scene 5 of the play by Shakespeare. Virginia Woolf's *A Room of One's Own* I have in the edition published by Mariner Books, edited by Mark Hussey, with an introduction by Susan Gubar, in 2005. Robert Bringhurst discusses literature's relation to the forms of the written word in the essay *The Solid Form of Language: An Essay on Writing and Meaning*, which was published as a beautifully made small book by Canada's Gaspereau Press in 2004. Harold Bloom revisits Max Weinreich in "The Glories of Yiddish," *New York Review of Books*, November 6, 2008. Walter J. Ong discusses the grapholect in *Orality and Literacy*, which I have in the Routledge New Accents edition of 2002.

HOLY WRIT

Jorge Luis Borges's "Library of Babel" is foundational for me; you can get Anthony Kerrigan's English version from the Grove edition of *Ficciones*, published in 1994. There's a lot of the Holy Bible in this section; my version is the *Oxford Study Bible: Revised English Bible with the Apocrypha*, edited by M. Jack Suggs and Katherine Doob Sakenfeld (Oxford University Press, 1992). Northrop Frye discusses scripture and writing in *The Great Code: The Bible and Literature* (Mariner, 2002). Richard and Mary Rouse explore the meanings of *exarare* in "The Vocabulary of Wax Tablets," *Harvard Library Bulletin* n.s., vol. 1, no. 3 (Fall 1990). The Vulgate Bible is available in many online editions; I use the one produced at the University of Chicago (http://www.lib.uchicago.edu/efts/ARTFL/public/bibles/

vulgate.search.html). Saint Jerome discusses shorthand and dictation in his "Epistle CXVII, Letter to a Mother and Daughter Living in Gaul." This version comes from the *Select Letters of St. Jerome*
in the Heinemann edition published in 1933, with translation by F.
A. Wright. Harold Bloom discusses the authorship of the Jahwist
in *The Book of J* (Random House, 1991). Maimonides's discussion
of the "temptations of idolatry" is found in *The Reasons of the Laws
of Moses, from the More Nevochim of Maimonides,* by James Town-
ley (London, Longman, 1827). I develop my interpretation of Paul's
Epistles from reading the version in the *Oxford Study Bible,* with
help from *Paul and First-Century Letter Writing: Secretaries, Composition and Collection* by E. Randolph Richards (IVP Academic,
2004). The Oxyrhynchus papyri have been published since 1898
by the Egypt Exploration Fund, a project of scholarly editing that
continues today. For Carmen 1 of Catullus's and Martial's epigrams,
4.10 and 1.29, I consulted in the Latin via Project Perseus; the translations are mine. T. C. Skeat's take on the codex can be found in *The
Collected Biblical Writings,* edited by J. K. Elliott, published by Brill
in 2004. Origen's impact on scribal tradition is discussed magiste-
rially in Anthony Grafton and Megan Williams, *Christianity and
the Transformation of the Book: Origen, Eusebius, and the Library of
Caesarea* (Harvard, 2006).

LOGOS EX MACHINA

The snippet of JavaScript is part of the codebase for Library Observa-
tory, a project developed by my research group, metaLAB at Harvard,
for the Digital Public Library of America. The code is open source,
meaning it's freely available for reuse, revision, and repurposing. Like
much programming for the web it is a kind of palimpsest, with links
to, and glimmers of, code from a variety of open public repositories;

its formulation was chiefly the work of my metaLAB colleague Jessica Yurkofsky. The single line of BASIC code gets its close reading in *10 PRINT CHR$(205.5+RND(1)); : GOTO 10* by Nick Montfort, Patsy Baudoin, John Bell, Ian Bogost, Jeremy Douglass, Mark C. Marino, Michael Mateas, Casey Reas, Mark Sample, and Noah Vawter; it's part of the Software Studies series edited by Matthew Fuller, Lev Manovich, and Noah Wardrip-Fruin (MIT Press, 2013). My consideration of Bening's book practice is developed from reading *Introduction to Manuscript Studies* by Raymond Clemens and Timothy Graham (Cornell University Press, 2007) and M. D. Reeve, "Manuscripts Copied from Printed Books," in *Manuscripts in the Fifty Years After the Invention of Printing*, J. B. Trapp, ed. (Warburg Institute, 1983). My discussion of rotunda and batarde scripts is in dialogue with Sheila Edmunds, "From Schoeffer to Vérard," in *Printing the Written Word*, Sandra L. Hindman, ed. (Cornell University Press, 1992), 30. My understanding of the role of punch cutting in the transition from manuscript to type depends crucially on Fred Smeijers, *Counterpunch: Making Type in the Sixteenth Century, Designing Typefaces Now* (Hyphen Press, 2nd ed., 2011). My translation of Pope Pius II's letter about "that marvelous man" Gutenberg is based on the version found in Martin Davies, "Juan de Carvajal and Early Printing: The 42-Line Bible and the Sweynheym and Pannartz Aquinas," *The Library* 6:XVIII, no. 3, September 1996. The Caxton quote appears in the preface (page ii) of *The Boke of Eneydos*, translated and with a preface by William Caxton, printed by Caxton not before June 23, 1490. The full title of the work is *Here fynyssheth the boke yf Eneydos, compyled by Vyrgyle, which hathe be translated oute of latyne in to frenshe, and oute of frenshe reduced in to Englysshe by me wyll[ia]m Caxton, the xxij. daye of Iuyn. the yere of our lorde. M.iiij.Clxxxx. The fythe yere of the regne of kynge Henry the seuenth.* To source this passage, I used the electronic edition from Early English Books Online (Ann Arbor, University of Michigan), which reproduces a copy of the original held by the British Library. The translation, from Caxton's early-modern English, is mine. Robert Braham is quoted by Tim William Machan in *Caxton's Trace: Studies in the History of English Printing*, William Kuskin, ed. (Notre Dame, 2006), 312–13. The account of the Star Chamber, *Libellis famosis*, and the Puritan Press is developed in part by Marvin Olasky in *Central Ideas in the Development of American Journalism* (Routledge, 1990). Adrian Johns discusses the Statute of Anne in *The Nature of the Book: Print and Knowledge in the Making* (University of Chicago, 2000). Juliet Fleming explores Elizabethan graffiti in *Graffiti and the Writing Arts of Early Modern England* (Reaktion, 2009). Emerson's exhortation to write on doorposts is found in the essay "Self-Reliance." I find Robert Service's poem "The Telegraph Operator" at the website of the Poetry Foundation, http://www.poetryfoundation.org/poem/174351. Tom Jennings terrifically documents the development of ASCII from the Baudot code in his essay "An Annotated History of Some Character Codes," published online at http://worldpowersystems.com/archives/codes/#BAUDOT. Another excellent source is *The History of Telegraphy* by Ken Beauchamp (IEEE, 2001); and, for a grand contextualization of the telegraph, see James Gleick's *The Information* (Pantheon, 2011). My understanding of the transformation wrought in writing by computation emerges from a number of sources, including Jon Agar, *Turing and the Universal Machine: The Making of the Modern Computer* (Icon, 2001); Paul E. Ceruzzi's crucial *A History of Modern Computing* (MIT Press, 1998); and Martin Campbell-Kelly and William Aspray, *Computer: A History of the Information Machine* (Basic Books, 1996). Alan Turing is quoted from "Intelligent Machinery: National Physical Laboratory Report," in B. Meltzer and D. Michie, eds., *Machine Intelligence 5* (Edinburgh University Press, 1969); I rely on Turing's famous essay, "Computing Machinery and Intelligence," which appeared in *Mind* 59, no. 236 (October 1950): 433–60. The Unicode Standard

5.2.0, published online (http://www.unicode.org/versions/Unicode5 .2.0/), is the most recent version at the time of this writing. "An Introduction to Bitic Literature" is found in English in Stanisław Lem's *Imaginary Magnitude* (Mariner, 1985). Walter Benjamin's "Theses on the Philosophy of History" appears most familiarly in *Illuminations*, Hannah Arendt, ed. (Schocken, 1969). Random House has recently published a new edition of *The Art of Memory*, Frances Yates's classic study of mnemotechnics (2014). Nicholas Carr's contentious, brilliant book *The Shallows* appeared in 2011 under the Norton imprint. Maryanne Wolf considers the cognitive effects of changes in reading and writing techniques in *Proust and the Squid: The Story and Science of the Reading Brain* (Harper Perennial, 2008); Stanislas Dehaene's *Reading in the Brain: The New Science of How We Read* (Penguin, 2010) gives a tour of the current brain-science take on the ways of literacy. Carl Sagan discusses the *Voyager* and *Pioneer* plaques in *Murmurs of Earth: The Voyager Interstellar Record* (Random House, 1978). The LAGEOS probe's message is documented in NASA press release 76–67, April 13, 1976. David B. Givens discusses the challenge of writing and deep time in "From Here to Eternity: Communicating with the Distant Future," *ETC.: a Review of General Semantics* 39, no. 2 (Summer 1982): 159–79. And designs for conveying the danger of high-level nuclear-waste repositories are contained definitively in *Expert Judgment on Markers to Deter Inadvertent Human Intrusion into the Waste Isolation Pilot Plant*, Sandia Report SAND92–1382/UC–721, by Kathleen M. Trauth et al., prepared by Sandia National Laboratory for the U.S. Department of Energy, printed November 1993.

AFTERWORD: PAGE AS MIND

Thomas De Quincey's *Confessions of an English Opium-Eater* and *Suspiria de profundis* were published in Boston by Ticknor & Fields in 1850; I consulted the digital version of this edition prepared by the Internet Archive (https://archive.org/details/confessionsofeng 03dequ). Hugh Kenner considers technology and literature in *The Mechanic Muse* (Oxford University Press, 1988).

ILLUSTRATION CREDITS

Page 10: Amherst Manuscript #776, p. 2, Letters to Mr. and Mrs. E. J. Loomis. Courtesy the Emily Dickinson Collection, Amherst College Archives and Special Collections.

Pages 44–45: Emile Cartailhac and Henri Breuil, *La caverne d'Altamira à Santillane près Santander* (1906). Planche XVII. Photo: Harvard Library Imaging Services.

Page 54: Cylinder Seal: Deities and Worshipper. Harvard Art Museums/Arthur M. Sackler Museum, Gift of Edward Waters, 1958.51. Photo: Imaging Department © President and Fellows of Harvard College.

Page 60: "You" Covered Ritual Wine Vessel with Decoration of Confronting Birds. Harvard Art Museums/Arthur M. Sackler Museum, Bequest of Grenville L. Winthrop, 1943.52.107. Photo: Imaging Department © President and Fellows of Harvard College.

Page 74: A Compendium of Seals on Japanese and Chinese Calligraphy and Paintings (*Wakan shoga inshû*). Harvard Art Museums/Arthur M. Sackler Museum, Gift of Dr. Ernest G. Stillman, Class of 1908, 1975.8. Photo: Imaging Department © President and Fellows of Harvard College.

Page 140: Gospel of Thomas. Greek, MS Gr SM4367, Houghton Library, Harvard University.

Page 152: Ostraca (3168) Letter, second century CE. In Greek. 10 x 9.5 cm. MS Richardson 32, Houghton Library, Harvard University. Photo by the author.

Page 162: Livy. *Les décades*, manuscript (c. 1415–1430), MS Richardson 32, Houghton Library, Harvard University; and *Biblia Latina* vol. 1 (Mainz: Johann Gutenberg, ca. 1454), HEW Biblia Latina, Houghton Library, Harvard University.

Page 210: The *Pioneer* Plaque (1972) is a NASA image, and thus in the public domain. Downloaded from https://solarsystem.nasa.gov/multimedia/display.cfm?Category=Spacecraft&IM_ID=8683; accessed February 12, 2015.

INDEX

Page numbers in *italics* refer to illustrations.